They all played at Lords

by

Geoff Webb

Darf Publishers

FIRST PUBLISHED 1991

ISBN 1 85077 218 5 (Hardcased)
ISBN 1 85077 223 1 (paperback)

Printed in Great Britain by BPCC Wheatons Ltd., Exeter
Cover design by Sue Sharples

They all played at Lords

Acknowledgements

THE author and publishers would like to thank Editor Michael Blumberg for giving his kind permission to reproduce some of the biographies already used by that excellent magazine CRICKET WORLD. The photographs were gathered from the archives of the Lords Museum and its helpful Curator, Stephen Green. This book is the result of many hours of typing by my understanding wife, Margaret, whose finished manuscripts are of the highest quality.

Dedicated to Margaret, Mark and Stuart.

List of Illustrations

Introduction

THIS collection of biographies contains players who entertained in the nineteenth century, with many continuing to savour the beginning of our present one. They have not been chosen on superiority, but simply to illustrate what characters the game boasted at that time. Sadly, cricket to-day, possibly because of its highly commercialised structure, does not throw up such personalities readily.

The list does not include outstanding criketers like W. G. Grace, Prince Ranjitsinhji, Lord Harris or Archie MacLaren, but this is intentional as they have been written of so copiously by others. I have concentrated on a cross section of their contemporaries, so important when assessing their considrable contributions to the game's early framework.

Some of the names belong to natural comedians, the odd martinet or two, and certainly to a band of unique captains, but predominant in all their qualities is that of giving over one hundred per cent effort on behalf of their team's performance. In their heyday, such household names immediately brought forth exclamations of awe, and often smiles of endearment.

To emphasize more an unbiased selection, they will 'bat' in chronological order, and I will ask the umpire to call 'play!' as you join these stalwarts in the centre to discover their stories.

Preface

Up to the age of sixteen I had played cricket for Redbourn, and under a blazing June sun, had spent many enjoyable hours hitting and chasing balls over the close-cropped grass of our little ground, on the village common. I had been going to school at St. Albans, and was a member of the school first eleven in my last three years. My efforts had not gone unnoticed because an offer to join the St. Albans club came my way: an opportunity I jumped at. Coupled with a great deal of help and encouragement from playing colleagues and old mentors of the club, with that of having a large proportion of the rub of the green, I was eventually chosen to play for Hertfordshire. These were very exciting times for me, but I think the cricket that brought me the most enjoyment was when the Club Cricket Conference, after a trial game at Guildford, asked me to play for them over the next few years.

I have written the foregoing details of my early cricketing life at the risk of sounding very immodest, but it is necessary when I tell you, the reader, the contents of a letter delivered to me on a certain April morning in 1955. The opening paragraph read: "It is with pleasure that I have to advise you of your selection to play for the Club Cricket Conference against the M.C.C. at Lords, on Wednesday and Thursday, the 18th and 19th May, 1955." It didn't seem possible that I, a lad who had been playing on the common a few years before, had been asked to play at Lords, of all places. I suppose this is the dream of all club cricketers, and mine had come true. Lords had always been my favourite ground to watch Test Matches, and many times I had sat marvelling at Wally Hammond's stylish follow through, as the ball crashed into the fence behind extra cover. It was enthralling to watch the audacity of Dennis Compton as he stroked balls off his wicket to fine leg, with utter disdain. Sitting there watching these great players, I was just as capable as the next person of fantasizing that I would play on that wicket—one day.

For countless years my family had operated the local dairy, providing the villagers with their daily pintas, so when playing for Hertfordshire or St. Albans, it meant getting up that bit earlier in order to finish my milk rounds in time to get to 'away' matches. On this special occasion Dad, Ray my brother, and the other roundsmen kindly agreed to do my rounds for me, thus giving me two complete days off to concentrate on the game. Another reason was in the event of a mishap. Can you imagine telephoning Lords on the morning of the second day to say. "Sorry, but I shall have to cry off to-day as I have cut my hand on a broken milk bottle, while delivering early this morning." In hindsight I was fortunate this didn't happen during any of my County games.

About a week before the great day the M.C.C. published its side, and quite a line-up it provided. For this fixture each season the M.C.C. selected a few players from the County side not participating in the County Championship games being played at that time. For 'my' match Northants were the side without a game, so our opponents included Young, Brown, Bennett and Robins (captain) from Middlesex, Dr. C. B. Clark, the ex-West Indian leg-break and googly bowler, Bird, of Worcester, and Andrew, Brookes, Poole, Subba Row and Tyson, all from Northants. The prospect of facing up to Frank Tyson at Lords was of nerve-tingling proportion, for he had just arrived home from 'down under' after devastating the might of Australia's batting line-up with sheer speed, to help retain the Ashes.

As days slipped by the weather turned grim, with bitterly cold winds tempering spring's late emergence. My girl friend Margaret— now my wife—had visited the farm on the eve of the game, and when it was time to walk her home we opened the front door to an icy blast. A freak snow shower was blowing from the north, and swirling flakes raced to the far end of our hall; a bleak prospect for the morrow.

I arranged to travel up to Lords on the Green Line coach which passed through our village to Dorking, via St. John's Wood Road, but although the good wishes expressed by a few locals I met while walking to the bus stop were encouraging to my expectations, they did nothing to ease those butterflies beginning to make their presence felt. Arriving at Lords on previous visits, I mused, my bag contained sandwiches and pop, on this occasion I carried a much larger bag, full of cricket gear.

Approaching the pavilion, by passing along under the grandstand and Old Father Tyme, I noticed seagulls with hunched backs, resting on the outfield to brave the watery sunshine and keen breeze. Reaching the back door I was faced by an official who smilingly admitted me on the strength of my cricket bag and Conference tie, so different from the countless times I had waited outside this same door at the end of a day's play to collect autographs of famous players. To reach our dressing room meant climbing two short flights of stairs, each step sporting a gleaming brass tread plate. On the walls were old prints and team photographs, and immediately a feeling that all the old-time greats had passed up these very stairs, was most apparent. The dressing room was spacious, with comfortable easy chairs, a masseur's table, and spotless bath and shower facilities nearby. Having time to spare, it was pleasant sitting on the window balcony overlooking the ground, quietly discussing the forthcoming match and surroundings with other team members, a few of whom were also playing their first game at Lords.

When we lost the toss and were asked to field, I was glad of the opportunity to go out and get the feel of the ground, also to liberate some of the butterflies now waging war. Following skipper Leo Bennett downstairs we reached a door opening into the Long Room, where members stood about in groups quietly talking, or sat at vast tables idly scanning editions of The Times and The Observer. Some conversations were interrupted briefly while they scrutinized us rather closely, making our way to the front doors. Around the walls were still more paintings and photographs of past teams and celebrities, some of whom were revered names in their playing days, but kept busy now in cricket administration. Along the lower parts of the walls glass fronted cabinets displayed rows of ancient bats, of all shapes and sizes. The dark brown ones had been used by W. G. Grace and his contemporaries, not to mention the bow-shaped cudgels wielded by stars even before the Doctor's time. Passing through the front doors we emerged into the sunlight to descend a flight of steps to the famed white gate. Everything about Lords reeks of tradition and all that cricket stands for, and stepping onto the grass I was instantly aware of the notorious slope, so much more pronounced standing at the gate that at any other position around the perimeter.

There weren't many people present when play began, but as the sun generated more heat, others drifted in hoping to see the 'Typhoon' carry on where he had left off in Australia. Fielding down near the Tavern I remember seeing Henry Oscar, the popular stage and television actor, sitting in the sun with his tankard of ale, and puffing contentedly at a short curly pipe. At the back of the grandstand a powerful camera with a long lens was mounted on its tripod, ready to be mobilized when required. I knew the cameramen weren't there to film me, but it wasn't until later in the day that the purpose of their visit was revealed. Although Subba Row showed his future England potential with a well made 42, the M.C.C. declared at a meagre 117 for 7, leaving us just over an hour to bat in poorish light.

When Frank Tyson marked out his recently acquired shortened run—he still ran a considerable distance—to bowl the first over, the cameramen went into action to film him thundering in to bowl his expresses. With the fall of our second wicket at ten minutes past six I had to go in and face Frank Tyson, just starting his second short spell at the pavilion end. At the fall of a wicket at Lords the incoming batsman has to be prepared to start his journey to the crease immediately, otherwise he doesn't make it in time. Passing through the Long Room I was conscious of may pairs of eyes following my every step, and odd wishes of 'good luck!' seemed to come from far off, barely penetrating my dazed progress. It seemed an awfully long way to the wicket, and after taking a middle-and-leg guard from the umpire, Frank Tyson looked a long way from me too. Making an adequate mark as a block-hole I took the customary look around the field—that was another shock. Tyson was waiting in the distance busily wearing out the groin of his trousers polishing the ball, short leg was in a stooped position, while Walter Robins sauntered in at cover point: all the other fielders were behind me in an arc betwen backward short leg and gulley.

Now Frank Tyson is a gentle, softly spoken fellow, and having an intellectual tendency, likes nothing more that to sit quietly reading a volume of William Shakespeare's writings. At ten minutes past six that evening he was transformed into Mr. Hyde as he sped towards me, and reaching the wicket seemed to continue and bowl from about seventeen yards. With no reduction of pace in his run-up, he delivered the ball with a violent shoulder and arm action, culminating in a long follow through to almost shake hands with Walter Robins or myself. The first delivery I saw as a red blurr, where I imagined the ball to be, and thinking of the space through mid off, I pushed forward to take an easy single. I was so late on it that when I looked round Keith Andrew, the 'keeper, had whisked it to one of the slips, who was looking to return it to the bowler via Robins. I managed to make contact with the second ball, but unfortunately it was with the big toe on my right foot. It hit me full pitch, and the toe went completely numb, remaining that way until the middle of June! With the ball dead I nonchantly tended the wicket as if nothing untoward had happened, not that there was anything to attend to, then slowly made my way back to take my stance, trying to give the impression that everything was under control. Deciding to cut out any backlift, I began to put bat to ball, managing to see out the rest of the play until 6.30.

Thoughtfully changing afterwards I tried to recapture some of the highlights of an historic day—for me. A team photograph taken in front of the traditional rose covered trellis on a lawn at the rear of the pavilion; being pleasantly surprised at the professionals' friendly manner towards us lesser fry and the roast beef and Yorkshire pudding followed by peaches and fresh cream, we had for lunch. On the way home with my parents and friends we stopped for a welcome meal at a timbered restaurant, where we relaxed and talked about the eventful day, and laughed when Dad pointed out that sitting square to the wicket, he was unable to follow the flight of the ball when Tyson bowled: I had to agree it wasn't any easier being closer to him.

The next day I scraped together 29 runs before Don Bennett brought one back sharply to hit my off stump. Yes, I had left a gap big enough to get a football through. The Conference made 163 for 8 declared, and in the M.C.C.'s second innings of 177 for 3 declared, Subba Row again confirmed his class with a solid 77. By playing out time on 85 for 6 we achieved quite a creditable draw, but my second innings contribution was precisely nil, because Jack Young straightened one and trapped me plum in front.

The following year I had the good fortune to play in the same fixture, and reaped a little more success against an attractive M.C.C. side that included the Sussex stars Jim Parks, Alan Oakman and Ian Thomson. This same season, 1956, happened to be part of the Club Cricket Conference's centenary year, and again I was lucky enough to be selected for a special Centenary match at the Oval against the touring Australians, who that summer, you will remember, had been severely 'Lakered'. His Royal Highness Prince Philip attended the match, dining with both teams, who mixed together in a most friendly manner. After lunch we were introduced to the Prince whose relaxed, informal conversation helped to create a homely atmosphere. Our day was memorable for many reasons, not the least being the interesting chats we had with the Aussies, but the biggest disappointment was the fact that rain poured down all day, thus preventing a ball from being bowled. For someone who had started his cricket with the postman bowling each day to him in the back yard, then graduating to the village club on the common, these major cricketing milestones remain indelible.

When cricketing celebraties write their memoirs, many of them recall an early ambition to play at Lords, so I think on May 18, 1955, I shared something of their feelings when their dreams were fulfilled.

CHAPTER ONE

William Clarke
(Notts C. C. C.) 1798–1856

IF William Clarke held the equivalent sway in to-day's cricket circles
as he did in the mid nineteenth century, he would be chairman of the
Test selectors, top of the bowling averages and the owner of Trent
Bridge! Such a despotic figure was born to a Nottingham bricklayer
and his wife on Christmas Eve, 1798. As a lad he followed in his
father's line of work, but cricket's history was influenced when he
married, too young some thought, and took the Bell Inn, soon to be
the cricketing centre of Nottingham. A son, Alfred, was born in
1831, and, under his father's captaincy, was to play for Nottinghamshire and the All England XI as a stylish batsman.

Upon the sad death of his wife, William Clarke soon married
again, and in hindsight, one is forgiven for thinking that business
possibilities of such a union may have out-weighed those of a more
amorous nature. You see, the new Mrs. Clarke just happened to be
Mary Chapman, manageress of the Trent Bridge Inn. 'Old' Clarke, as
he was affectionately known in later life, wasted no time in laying
down an enclosed cricket pitch, for which he charged 6d. admission.
Nottinghamshire had previously played on the Forest Ground, but
being common land, no entrance charge could be made. The new
ground was opened in 1838, and soon became the new home of
Nottinghams cricket. At first the sixpenny charge was unpopular with
the public, so much so that people jeered when Clarke started to
bowl, or went in to bat. In time they came to accept his, seemingly,
forthright actions and outlandish manner, but his superb bowling, not
to mention his maiden century on the ground in 1838 (125 for Holme
Lane v Bingham), finally won them over.

As a young man Clarke had been influenced by Tom Warsop, an
old Nottinghamshire bowler, who left an impression on the budding
cricketer to follow in his footsteps. William Clarke achieved this
ambition, when he made his early debut in 1816, as a 17 year old.
Even after receiving tuition concerning change of pace, from William

1

William Clarke 1848

Lambert, the Surrey allrounder, it was twenty years before Clarke made his first appearance at Lords, in a match for the North v the South, in 1836. He was 38 years old that year, the year, incidentally when bowlers were credited for wickets taken by stumping and catches in matches at Lords, but he wasn't to play there again until 1843.

At the age of 30 he had the misfortune to lose an eye, after being struck by the ball in a game of fives, a sport at which he was highly acclaimed. Although suffering from impaired vision, he played an important innings of 71 for Married v Single at Lords, in 1849, even against the bowling wiles of Wisden, Armitage and Martingell. He made several useful scores, but his batting, considering his disability and his prime love of bowling, never reached its full potential.

Due to a deformed arm, after breaking it in a fall, 'Old' Clarke delivered his lobs with an under-arm jerk at waist level. He could bowl fast or slow, and achieved a movement from leg to off, with a disconcerting lift from the wicket. Using the same action he obtained a clever change of pace, and many batsmen moved out to attack him, only to be left stranded. His menacing smile as he approached the wicket should have been ample warning, but they seemed to prefer suicide. Caffyn thought his faster ball was the more lethal in the latter mode of assault.

'Old' Clarke didn't practice before a game, but walked around the ground studying batsmen loosening up. He was a master at reading batsmen's defects, also those of the wicket. The Reverend Cannon M'Cormick was practising one day in the nets when he came under the scrutiny of William Clarke. Taking the ball Clarke gave the surprised striker an easy lob to drive, which he duly accepted. The bowler called George Anderson, a Yorkshire pro' batsman whom William coached, to field 20 yards behind him. Clarke bowled a similar ball, but the Reverend was easily caught after driving too early. The bowler was a master of field placing, but accuracy was his strong point. When 'Old' Clarke was matched with Felix in a single wicket game, Lord Bessborough inquired of the Notts man how he would dismiss such a talented batsman. The bowler illustrated his intentions by delivering seven high flighted balls, hitting the stump tops each time. The ploy quickly proved successful on match day.

If batsmen remained patient, Clarke could be played for long periods. William Clarke, always appearing tireless, as when trundling 64 successive balls to Pilch and Warman in an innings, without them scoring. He managed to do the same to Caffyn and Box in a later match. Such aimless methods of survival, although commendable to a point, never won matches. The alternative was never easy, for Fuller

Pilch, the leading batsman at this time, never mastered him over 30 years. Perhaps he should have read Felix's pamphlet "How to Play Clarke!" Being captain 'Old' Clarke was reluctant to rest, and, at the start of an innings, even told his bowling partner that he could have which end he liked—after Clarke had pointed out his preference! James Pycroft, the ancient historian, recalled how William Clarke would only bowl from the pavilion end at Lords, because the slope made his bowling break too sharply from the other end.

During the seasons between 1848 and 1854 he took 222, 267, 307, 343, 319 and 476 wickets respectively. Even considering they were obtained against teams of twenty-two and eighteen inexperienced cricketers in many cases, such returns are still remarkable. He bowled unchanged through both innings of a match on four occasions, and took eight or nine wickets in an innings five times, and 13 or more six times. These figures were achieved against leading teams of that era.

William Clarke's first game for the Gents *v* the Players was in 1846, at Lords, when he took five for 30 off nine overs, at the age of 47. The following year, after 19 ineffectual overs from Hillyer and Dean, Clarke, with Lillywhite finished off the Players innings by taking four for 26 and six for 18 respectively. In the second innings they bowled unchanged for five wickets each. Clarke again bowled unchanged through the game in 1850 and finished with 12 wickets, including the illustrious scalp of Alfred Mynn twice—and cheaply. In nine Gents matches he took 50 wickets at 11 runs each.

Also in 1846 he was engaged by the M.C.C. as a practice bowler at Lords, and suddenly came to people's notice as an outstanding potential. In this same monumental year his business acumen was made apparent when he took the cream of English cricket to form the travelling All England Eleven. The first game took place at the Hyde Park Ground at Sheffield, during August 1846. William Clarke retired from the Trent Bridge Inn in 1847 as his commitments to the A.E.E. now occupied all his time and thoughts. He had an amazing knowledge of cricket lore, together with visions of how the game would develop. People then thought him eccentric when suggesting a winter cricket school for practice. Many doubters visualised the advent of the A.E.E. to be the doom of cricket, but the opposite was, in fact, the outcome.

The team toured to all parts of the country by means of stage coaches, but the development of the railways helped to cut down such tedious travelling time, and more fixtures were made to play teams of XXII and XVIII. As a small boy, W. G. Grace was taken to see the A.E.E. at Bristol in 1854, when it played a local XXII organised by his father. Such awe imprinted on that young mind remained indelible. More people now were able to watch their heroes, and committees were formed to arrange receptions, while at coaching inns and railway stations the public assembled in their hundreds to cheer the arriving visitors. Some towns and villages actually rang their church bells in welcome. The hospitality was overwhelming to most of the players, but 'Old' Clarke only partook of a bottle of soda water and a cigar when playing, and consumed a whole goose at close of play! William Caffyn, in his book "71 Not Out", describes how he felt privileged just to ride with the A.E.E., and to be in their company.

The A.E.E. played in white shirts with small red spots or stripes, but this is not obvious in a drawing by Felix of the assembled team in its prime. Although Clarke was 5' 9" tall, and weighed 14 stones, he is dwarfed by Alfred Mynn. William Clarke looks very dapper in high waisted, white trousers, a tall shirt collar with a black choker tied in a bow, black shoes, and a large grey topper with a wide black band. His astute cricket brain was illustrated when selecting his team, for he always chose his wicket-keeper first, irrespective of the player's batting ability. He even had a say in the opposition's selection as shown when he objected to the Surrey quickie, Tom Sherman playing on a rough wicket, and battering his stars. The objection was sustained. 'Old' Clarke was the sole selector for the England side when playing such leading counties as Kent and Sussex, also for the North when playing the South eleven.

Often referred to as "the General" by his players, 'Old' Clarke was a strict disciplinarian, and expected each one to give his all—and possibly more. If a successful player's performance was recognised by a gift of money from an admirer, Clarke expected to receive a part of it: there were no arguments if the recipient wished to play for the A.E.E. again! His humour, although sometimes cruel, caused many a laugh. A doting mothing, hoping to gain a place in the team for her son, approached 'Old' Clarke confidently, and explained, "He's six feet in his stockings"! The skipper, with an extra twinkle in his good eye, replied "Dear me,what a lot of toes he must have"! As William Clarke aged, his temper grew shorter and, with some players agitating to reform the poor wages he paid them, the boat was being rocked. It was common knowledge that Clarke was a wealthy person, his affluent status considerably aided by the returns of A.E.E. matches.

Like wine, his cricket improved with age, for his best was seen in his last ten years. 'Old' Clarke took 2,385 wickets for the A.E.E., and, although many were taken in games versus teams of odds, he was the master of all leading batsmen of that period. He kept a diary of his playing days, but, sadly it was lost: it would have thrown light on many aspects of cricket's infancy.

Those tell tale cracks in morale finally opened when fourteen players broke away from the A.E.E. in 1852, to form a new touring team called the United England Eleven. Led by Johnny Wisden, the rebels included such stars as Dean, Tom Adams, John Lillywhite, Tom Lockyer, Jemmy Grundy and Tom Sherman. The cricket public clamoured for the two teams to meet, but 'Old' Clarke was adamant that they should not, and they didn't while he was living.

William Clarke died at Priory Lodge, Wandsworth, London, in 1856, at the age of 57. He was buried in Northwood Cemetery. In his latter years severe throat ailments, and fits, had plagued him to the end. Such hindrances didn't stop him from taking a wicket with the last ball he bowled, just two months before his death. It was for the A.E.E. versus a twenty-two of Whitehaven. George Parr, one of Clarke's 'discoveries', succeeded "the General" as manager of the A.E.E. and, very soon, the two leading teams did meet, regularly. It was George Parr who had affectionately remarked how 'Old' Clarke played more by ear than by sight, later in his career!

However long the game is played, William Clarke, the 'father' of Nottinghamshire cricket, will be remembered as one of its leading characters, and players.

CHAPTER TWO

Alfred Mynn
(Kent & England) 1807–1861

ALFRED Mynn, from pure Kentish yeoman stock, was the first cricketer to be idolised nationally in the game's comparative infancy. His magnificent physique and genial personality brought him a following not only of youngsters, who eagerly clamoured at his heels, but also the adult public who doted on his every move. Splendidly proportioned at 6ft.1in. and weighing eighteen stones, he towered over his fellow players.

Born at Twisdon Lodge, Gourdhurst, Kent in 1807 Alfred first played cricket at nearby Harrietsham when he was 18 years old. It was at this time that John Willes had been campaigning for the legislation of shoulder-height deliveries which Alfred's ability and popularity helped to bring to fruition. When reminiscing, old cricketers enjoyed recalling how Alfred moved majestically in to bowl his expresses, normally from the position of round the wicket; the ball would move off the pitch from leg-stump to off. Even during this explosive period of cricket evolution Alfred Mynn's fairness of delivery was never questioned.

Alfred's batting was always entertaining. His powerful driving and hitting on the leg-side was executed with graceful movements and a natural eye. His bat appeared toy-like in his enormous hands and he always looked more comfortable against fast bowling than slow—this was due to his range of shots lacking variety. Hillyer and Redgate, the other two fast bowlers of this era, rated Alfred as the most dangerous hitter they encountered. When fielding he would be stationed at short slip and one of his leg-of-mutton hands was considered sufficient to hold any catch offered in his direction.

On December 15, 1828 Alfred Mynn married Sarah Powell at Trinity Church, Newington. This union was to be blessed with five daughters in quick succession. During this busy period Alfred joined the Leeds Club and played his first game in 1829, but with little success.

The year 1833 provides the first milestone in Alfred's cricket career

Alfred Mynn

when he was selected, from virtual obscurity, for the Gentlemen against the Players at Lords on August 27 and 28. Although the Gentlemen lost by an innings, Alfred Mynn bowled four and had one caught. he really began to make his mark at this point, for he was now playing with the Gentlemen of Kent and rapidly proving himself the leading Kent amateur. Kent played their County games at Chislehurst, and near the end of this season the Kent Gentlemen took on the might of the Gentlemen of England. The latter won the game by nine runs, but, even with this jump to a higher standard, Alfred still managed to bowl out three in the first innings and four in the second.

Some cricket writers have assessed the Kent team from the middle 1830's through to 1850 as the greatest County XI of all time. With such favourites as wicket-keeper Wenman, Hillyer, and Norfolk born Fuller Pilch this side was always well supported, and it meant large gates wherever they played. Walter Mynn, an elder brother, was captain but seldom was he referred to in cricket literature.

In 1834 Alfred Mynn played for the first time with Felix, the Surrey artist-schoolmaster, who later joined the great Kent XI and was to become a life-long friend. Sussex and Surrey had been the leading counties, but now Kent started to overcome all opposition.

When stumpings and catches were credited to the bowlers for the first time in 1836, Alfred's averages were greatly improved. He played for the M.C.C. that year as a given man—this was indeed an unusual event as they generally selected teams from their wealthy members only. Against Sussex, at Brighton he scored 45 well made runs in the first innings and when, after one huge hit, the blade of the bat parted company from its handle, he completed his runs by touching down with just the handle. The second innings brought even greater deeds from him—92 runs, being his largest score in cricket so far. Sussex ended up seven runs short and Alfred bowled nine batsmen in the match.

Earlier that year there had been rumblings from the North of a forthcoming challenge to the South. It was arranged to play the first game at Lords, which the North won by six wickets, with the return at Leicester, starting on August 22. Practising before the start at Leicester, Alfred hit a ball hard on to the inside of his right ankle, but, with the aid of a runner was able to score a good 21 not out. Playing for the North was Redgate who, with Mynn, were at that time the fastest bowlers in England. In the second innings Alfred was struck many times on the inside of his right leg by Redgate, but after five hours he was unbeaten with a chanceless 125: the only century he ever made. The South won this game by 218 runs—but at what cost? As Alfred Mynn staggered from the wicket he was met by Lord Frederick Beauclerk, who, on seeing the condition of Alfred's leg, was aghast that Alfred could even stand. A fly was called for to take Alfred to his lodgings and from there he was quickly taken to board the stage-coach to London. Due to his bulk and the very stiff leg they were unable to accommodate him inside the coach so he was safely secured on top. After a long arduous journey over the rough roads to London, he was too ill to go on to Kent, so he stayed at the Angel's Tavern in St. Martin's Lane. Alfred was moved to St. Bartholomews Hospital where doctors deliberated deeply over whether or not to amputate the limb. Alfred was adamant that they must not do this. It is not clear how long he stayed in Hospital, but it was nearly two years before he played again.

This was a sad period of Alfred Mynn's life for in 1837 both his parents died. After moving house to Thurnham, Sarah at last produced a son but unfortunately he only lived for two hours. She was again successful in 1843, only for the infant to die after six weeks.

It was at about this time that pads and gloves appeared for the batsmens' protection from the dangers of Redgate and Mynn, and it was thought that Alfred used padded protection inside his trousers when he resumed playing in 1838. Frederick Gale recalls that a pair of Alfred's pads were presented to W. G. Grace at the beginning of his illustrious career. Lord Harris tells of a pair of Mynn's pads that were kept in the Canterbury pavilion, and of what poor protection they must have provided.

Alfred Mynn's next game for the Gentlemen was against the Players in 1839. This was to be the first of 14 consecutive appearances, with the Gentlemen winning five times to the Players three. With his tremendous speed and a little help from the notoriously rough wickets of this era Alfred took wickets regularly. Many prominent players told about the audible hum of the ball as it left Alfred's hand. Two long-stops were not uncommon to help the brave, overworked wicket-keepers, and one second long-stop, after being hit in the chest by one of Alfred's thunderbolts, was reported to have spat blood for a fortnight.

Batting in the second innings of the 1842 Gents versus Players match Alfred scored a solid 46, but received another blow on his old injury. With the assistance of a dozen leeches the swelling was reduced, enabling Alfred to bowl out six batsmen in the second innings.

The 1843 match was highlighted by the one-handed stumping of G. Butler by the Gentlemen's wicket-keeper T. A. Anson from one of Alfred's tremendous shooters. He was noted for being ambidextrous, for once he stumped a batsman with his right hand and, in one movement, caught the bail with his left and replaced it. The batsman was surprised to be given out when he looked round to see the wicket intact.

The first averages were produced in 1840 for batsmen only, but not until 1843 were bowlers incorporated, with Alfred Mynn heading the bowlers' tables for the first three years. These firgures were not considered to be very reliable until Bell's Life, in 1846, produced their own sets of averages for both batsmen and bowlers, and Alfred always figures prominently in both.

Kent first played at Canterbury in 1841 against England, and this was the birth of the Canterbury week. The next game, in 1842, resulted in a win for England by 74 runs, with Alfred taking eleven wickets in the match. Ugly whispers from the losing Kentish 'punters' suggested that the Kentish players sold the game—the next time Alfred Mynn walked into Maidstone market he was hissed. Connecting Alfred with something underhand seems unlikely, for Felix once told the Rev. Pycroft of an occasion when a certain Baronet approached Alfred with an unsporting offer. The Kent idol instantly snapped "Get out of my sight or, Baronet as you are, I am sure I shall be knocking you down."

Gambling at cricket was commonplace and many cricketers, like prize fighters, had their own backers. Alfred Mynn's chief patron was Lord Frederick Cavendish. Single wicket cricket was very popular at this period and provided the gentry with ample opportunities to back their fancies. Alfred, with his wonderful all round ability, was soon a popular and successful performer. After overcoming other competent single wicket cricketers, he stepped into Fuller Pilch's place when James Dearman, of Sheffield, issued a challenge to the latter in 1838. The Yorkshireman was overwhelmed in this and the return game, only for Alfred to be recognised from then on as "Champion of England" at single wicket cricket. Eight years later he was challenged by his close friend Felix, although this seemed hardly feasible as he was a batsman who depended on deflections to score his runs. The rules of the single wicket game stated that only shots in front of the wicket counted, and one foot had to be anchored behind the crease. The normal two runs only counted as one so the fact that Felix was the challenger caused speculative interest. In the first game Felix opened the batting and survived for three hours, receiving 262 balls and hitting 186 of them. A very commendable effort indeed but unfortunately he only totalled 4 runs, and Alfred knocked them off after just 16 balls.

When a public figure of such giant proportions and amiable character is so successful 'titles' automatically follow, and Alfred was typically dubbed as "Lion of Kent", "Alfred the Great", "The Great Man of Kent" and "The Kentish Giant". Such tags have to be lived up to, and Alfred was never known to show any animosity towards his fellow players. On one occasion at Lords, Felix was standing at point and dropped a catch off Alfred's bowling. Felix was always looking to cause laughter with funny antics and this time he chose to fall in a squat position, with head down and arms folded around his knees. Alfred walked down the wicket and, with one hand gripping the human "ball" by the collar of his flannel jacket, held up the joker at arms length. Arthur Haygarth, the compiler of Scores & Biographies, was present and refers to Alfred Mynn's abnormal strength, for Felix, although being short and stocky, weighed around eleven stones.

Among the ranks of leading batsmen of this period were two amateurs who were more successful against Alfred than others. First was William Ward who handled the speed of Alfred Mynn from 22 yards more easily by having professionals bowl at him from 19 yards. The other batsman was the Hon. Robert Grimston who solved the problem by taking two bats to the crease. When facing the other bowlers he used a light one, and when Alfred was rocketing them down he used the heavier one, which he called "Mynn's Master".

The 1845 season was an unfortunate one for Alfred, but mainly from a financial angle. His name was missing from games in the first half of the season and rumours of his imprisonment for debts were not all unfounded. A document in Kent County Council archives records his bankruptcy, followed by a jail sentence. It appears that an official body arrived with a warrant for his arrest during the game between The Western Counties and M.C.C., but he was allowed to finish only to be taken to Wilton Jail afterwards. Alfred's occupation was described as a Hop Merchant, but there is a suspicion that the Officials were confused with his brother, who was of that trade. Alfred was generally looked upon as a very suspect amateur, as he was able to play cricket regularly and still support a large family. However, he always retained his strong following of wealthy people who gambled heavily on his games. It is reasonable to assume that these supporters paid his bailment at the courts enabling him to miss so little cricket.

During 1846 the celebrated Nottinghamshire cricketer William Clarke formed the All England XI and, apart from playing, Alfred Mynn was elected as a member of the managing committee—was this another source of finance? Alfred generally batted low in the order but played a few good innings. Alas, he seldom bowled. With the advent of the railway, the touring All England XI was entertained lavishly by society all over England. This high living standard appealed to Alfred, as he often stated how he normally existed on beef and beer and once, when asked what else he trained on he smiled and said "beer and beef!" Cricket artist Corbet Anderson tells of the time Alfred sat for him to paint his portrait. The sitting lasted for two and a half hours, during which Alfred consumed two meals, each consisting of two and a half pounds of beef and a quart of beer. Ale seems to have been a constant lubrication for tuning this massive cricket machine.

When Butler Parr, a Nottinghamshire maltster and brewer, entertained the All England XI at his home Alfred would never drink his beer from a large glass. He always used two small ones with one constantly kept full. He was known to take ale to bed with him, and even when asleep Alfred could not be kept quiet. Richard Draft recalls how Alfred's thunderous snoring from an adjoining room kept him awake all one night. On another occasion when Alfred was staying in an hotel, a four poster bed collapsed under his enormous weight in the middle of the night.

Alfred Mynn was given a benefit match in 1847 when Kent met England at Lords on July 26 and 27. His popularity and the possibility of outstanding debts were the reasons he was granted this welcome gesture. He bowled seven of the Englishmen in their first innings and hit 48 out of 70 in Kent's first innings. When Alfred made the winning hit for Kent the large crowd was jubilant. Due to the leading players participating, and a forceful, hard working committee, the sum raised was believed to be quite large, but it was never revealed.

By 1848 the point was frequently made by journalists and others that Pilch, Felix and Alfred Mynn were 'over the top' and too old—Alfred had now reached the 'ripe old age' of 40, and weighed around 22 stones. Certainly, by 1852 the Kent side began to decline in stature and Alfred was bowling less and less.

The year 1851 was a particularly sad one for the genial Alfred as two close members of the family died, and in March he tragically lost his second daughter Mary Ann, aged 20. Nine months later his fourth daughter, Eliza Susannah, suddenly passed away after having been institutionalised. Alfred was a religious man and this must have been a most wretched time for him. This religious tendency was recalled by Felix who told of Alfred praying when the surgeons were debating whether to amputate a leg at the time of his injury. Felix also refers to the presence of Alfred's prayer book at their lodgings when on tour.

Up to 1856 he played only spasmodically, and because connected with the Southgate Club—later to become Middlesex C.C.C.—which was founded by the Walker brothers. His friendship with the Walkers was unbounded, but it was well known that he, and other deserving cases, received financial aid from this generous family.

William Hillyer was the other great fast bowler for Kent during

Alfred's playing days, and was granted a benefit match because of premature retirement through ill health. It was arranged that an England XI would play 18 veterans at the Oval in August, 1858. A short, but reminiscent, stand by Alfred and his old colleague, E. G. Wenman was ended with the latter's dismissal. As he passed, Alfred grasped his hand and said "Goodbye, my fellow cricketer. We have played many a happy match together and now our career is over". The veterans lost the game but a welcome £400 was raised for Hillyer and his family.

Playing a few games for Southgate and umpiring for the All England XI brought Alfred up to a turning point in Kent cricket history. He was a member of a body who formed the new Kent County Cricket Club in 1859 because of dissatisfaction with the old club: he was duly made a committee member. This same year Alfred joined the recently formed group of Leeds and Hollingbourne Volunteers to help combat the huffing and puffing of Napoleon III from across the English Channel.

In early January, 1861, William Hillyer died aged 47 and Alfred, together with his brothers Walter and Edgar Willsher, followed the coffin to their friend's early grave. Later that year English cricket lovers were saddened to hear of Alfred's own sudden death, caused by diabetes. There had been no hint of ill health when he died, aged 54, at Walter's house in Merrick Square, but the game had lost one of its great attractions. The Nation mourned and, when Felix was informed of Alfred's death, he wrote "One of the noblest specimens of manliness and courage combined with all that was becoming in a man". Many were the heartfelt tributes paid to him by the scribes and players of the game, but suitably summed up by one ". . . he was a great and lovable man to have known".

Alfred Mynn was given a military funeral by his comrades of the Volunteer Group and as the rain poured down three volleys were fired over his grave. Under a yew tree in a corner of Thurnham churchyard a solid headstone tells of Alfred's many attributes and also of the Trust set up to help pay for the stone. With contributions steadily pouring in, a committee was formed to distribute the surplus funds to deserving cases of Kent cricketers who had fallen on hard times.

In Memorium, written by the then promising sports writer W. J. Prowse, illustrated the loss to English society by the death of Alfred Mynn in admirably descriptive verse. The last line sums up the lament of Alfred's aggrieved followers for their hero. "Lightly lie the turf upon thee, kind and manly Alfred Mynn".

CHAPTER THREE

E. G. Wenman
(Kent C.C.C.) 1803–1879

USING careful, but firm strokes with a spoke-shave, Ned skilfully shaped a rough piece of ash to replace the rotted spoke of a cart-wheel, brought into his workshop that morning by a local farmer friend. Sawdust and shavings littered the floor, while dust particles spiralled through slanting sun-rays, which had managed to force their way through partly cobwebbed windows. Ned, a wheelwright and carpenter by trade, felt happier when out in sunlit, green Kentish fields, leading the invincible Kent eleven to inevitable victory.

Edward Gower Wenman, better known as Ned, was born in Benenden on 18th August, 1803, and was the first in a string of celebrated wicket keepers the county produced with unfailing regularity. Herbert Jenner-Fust followed Ned, while later Fred Huish, Leslie Ames, Godfrey Evans and Alan Knott were succeeded by Paul Downton, before he moved to Middlesex. Early records of the Benenden Club were not saved, so Ned's initial performances were missing from statiticians tables. He played his first game for Kent in 1825, when it was immediately obvious that a rare potential had been discovered.

Old prints show Ned Wenman's stance, from the bowler's view-point, with his left foot slightly forward, his hands held just above stump high. Crouched like a boxer, and towards the leg side, he is dressed in high-waisted trousers, with shoulder straps, his buttoned shirt with puffed sleeves fastened at the wrist. Shiny black shoes are in keeping with a high silk hat. Frederick Lillywhite's Scores and Biographies do not mention Ned's garb, but it is recorded there how he made his Lords debut in the Gents v Players match of 1829. To make it in such a prestigious fixture was considered quite remarkable.

At this time it was not uncommon for wicket keepers to bowl, for they had no encumbrances, such as pads and gloves to discard before doing so. Ned was no mean performer, and bowled for Kent and the Players, on several occasions. His action was described as ". . . a kind

E. G. Wenman

of high underhand". Wicket keepers wore no protection until Alfred Mynn hurled down his expresses on those notoriously rough wickets: still Ned wore neither pads nor goves. With Mynn and Hillyer bowling Ned had to endure great pain, his hands being cut and badly damaged. In 1836 the Reverend Pycroft recalls seeing Ned Wenman wearing one glove, lined with dog-skin, possibly, to protect an injury.

The art of 'keeping', in cricket's infancy, was so different from that of the present century. Two of the most important fielding positions were long-stop, and second long-stop—places reserved for the best fielders. Wicket keepers were only expected to stop balls thought worthy of the chore. During one Kent game Ned made a reference about his long-stop to the slip fielders. "What's the use of Walter Mynn for long-stop, if I am to do all his work and knock my hands to pieces? No, let him do his work, and I will do mine".

It was usual for wicket keepers to take the ball one-handed, and attempt stumping in the same action, but Ned was unique, because he used either hand equally well. Restricting byes to a minimum was not an important factor, as it is to-day. In Kent's match with Sussex, at Town Malling, in 1836, there were 51 byes out of a total of 348 runs. This was not regarded as unusual, even with Ned Wenman 'keeping' for Kent and Thomas Box for Sussex. In the same year, Kent played two games against Town Malling, which produced 113 extras in one match, and 110 in the other: Ned 'kept' on both occasions. For such a large framed man—he was 6ft. tall and weighed 15 stones—it was remarkable how he attempted stumpings while standing up to Mynn, Redgate and Hillyer. With the ball often shooting along the ground, or rearing head high, he was remembered for stumping batsmen off the extreme pace of Redgate in certain Gents v Players games.

Fuller Pilch, Ned's Kent colleague, told author Frederick Gale how Ned would watch the batsman's feet closely, and was rarely turned down for a stumping appeal, because of his good judgment. Sussex's Thomas Box was rated Ned's equal in some circles, if not better, but those two wily campaigners, Herbert Jenner-Fust and William Lillywhite thought Ned to be more reliable. Jenner-Fust, Wenman and Box were recognised as "the pioneers of the great school of wicketkeeping to fast bowling".

Although naturally left handed Ned batted right, and scoring many useful runs, was regarded a consistent performer. He was predominantly a back-foot player, with a punishing late-cut, very similar to George Parr's batting technique. From 1829 to 1846 Ned played seventeen times in the Gents v Players matches—once as a 'given' man for the Gents—and ended with a respectable average of 17.43.

The first of his two big innings for the Players was a 58 in 1839, and 73 out of 137 in 1843. After twenty five years service for Kent, from 1825 to 1854, his average of 11 was highly rated: he played but very little in the last 10 years. On one occasion against Sussex he equalled his highest score with a valuable 73, when Kent were struggling. Remembering those fearful wickets, how does one measure three such innings in value, compared with three of the same score made by a present day batsman, on his expertly nurtured strips? An example of how the rough wickets restricted the scoring rate was evident when Clarke and Day played for England against Kent at Cranbrook, in 1851. They bowled 32 overs at Fuller Pilch and Ned Wenman without conceding a run, and this was not considered a rare occurrence.

The great Kent eleven of the mid 1830's and early 1840's consisted of top performers in their particular spheres. Fuller Pilch and Felix were both superb batsmen, while Alfred Mynn and William Hillyer formed, probably, the fastest attack in the country. Ned Wenman was in the top bracket of wicket-keepers, and his positive leadership was far seeing, and utterly respected. The spirit of any successful side is naturally high, and in Ned's team there was no hint of jealousy, or bad feeling. Pilch described it as a team of brothers, because players' relationships were so cordial. Ned had great qualities as a leader, and, without loud commands or arm-waving, the players, Felix tells us, knew where to move when the skipper looked in their direction. There was always a word of encouragement for anyone going through a bad patch, and youngsters were helped to improve their game through his tactful and knowledgeable suggestions. His presence at a match served as a boost to bring in the crowds, not to mention the effect on betting odds. If Ned was injured, or indisposed when England played Kent, as they did quite often, the punters received longer odds on the National side. On one such occasion Felix overheard a nobleman confiding to a friend the fact that Wenman was absent, so they should back England—England won by 76 runs. Officials and fellow players always showed Ned genuine respect, wherever he played, and was once referred to "as the fairest cricketer that ever lived", When compiling data for his book 'The Game of Cricket', Frederick Gale chatted to Fuller Pilch, who said, when describing Mynn's bowling accuracy, ". . . he could put a ball on a sixpence, and he did just what Ned Wenman told him".

Benenden was the strongest club side in Kent, and the Wenman family provided the county with seven players between 1807 and 1864. Ned has three giant sons, but, much to his disappointment, only one played a few games for Kent. Perhaps it was about this time when Lord Harris met Ned and Walter Mynn during a Canterbury Week, and described them as ". . . large, silent men".

When it was announced, in 1843, that a benefit match for Ned Wenman would be played on August 17 and 18 between England and Kent, many leading players seized the opportunity to offer their services, in respect for a very popular colleague. The venue was near Benenden, at the Hampstead Park home of Mr. T. L. Hodges, a prominent Kent supporter. After Alfred Mynn had had match figures of 11 for 39, ensuring a 99 run Kent victory, Ned's wonderful day was rounded off with a dinner for both teams—all in his honour.

Ned Wenman was past 50 when he retired from competitive cricket, and not long afterwards, it was revealed that he had met with financial difficulties. The heady years of Kent success had taken their toll. Team mates, Mynn and Pilch, had also been guilty of spending too much time from their businesses, which naturally suffered by their absence. Possibly, Ned had seen the warning earlier, because he dropped out of cricket for a whole year in 1845, to concentrate on business affairs. Although outstanding for his organisation as a match manager, unfortunately, he lapsed when dealing with private commitments.

When Kent County Cricket Club was formed in 1859, Alfred Mynn and Ned Wenman, being two of the county's greatest cricketers, were elected to serve on the new committee. Such committees were normally comprised of leading county figures, noted, primarily, for their prominent social standing, backed by considerable wealth. It was thought that Ned found this sudden rise in his living status too much to cope with, and, after only 18 days in office, he announced that he "preferred not to act", and stood down.

Even in the twilight years of such an illustrious career, Ned never lost the spirit for a genuine challenge. In 1875, just four years before his death, Ned, aged 71, and his cousin, John Wenman, 71, joined with Richard Mills, 73, and issued a £100 challenge to any three in England, averaging the same number of years: the challenge was never taken up. Perhaps the cricket fraternity had long memories, for way back in 1834 Ned and Mills, also a Benenden stalwart, played an XI from the Isle of Oxney, at Wittersham—and defeated them by 66 runs. Ned took 13 wickets in the match, and scored 65 in the first innings.

At his Benenden home, on December 28, 1879, Ned Wenman died peacefully. His sporting demeanour, competitive, yet mild, manner was a combination seldom encountered in any walk of life; regrettably, it still is.

CHAPTER FOUR

George Parr
(Notts. C.C.C.) 1826–1891

To follow William Clarke as manager, captain and secretary of the All England Eleven was a daunting task, but commencing in 1856, George Parr fulfilled the posts manfully. The rise of Notts cricket, under the leadership of Parr, left no-one in doubt as to his effect on the side, both as skipper and player. Taking over the mantle of England's leading professional batsman from Fuller Pilch was another accomplishment nobody questioned. Such batting expertise remained unchallenged until the advent of W. G. Grace himself.

George Parr's parents were respected members of the farming fraternity around Radcliffe-on-Trent, and he was born in such pastoral surroundings on May 22, 1826. There were nine children in the family, and brother Sam, six years George's senior, was a Notts player for some years. Another long serving Notts stalwart, Butler Parr, was not related. George Parr played his first senior cricket as a fourteen year old lad for his local Radcliffe team, and it was there that 'Old' Clarke noted such an outstanding young talent, that he asked the youngster to play at Trent Bridge. It wasn't long before George Parr received his baptism in higher cricket in the Notts v. Leicestershire match at Trent Bridge, in 1845, and made a promising 24 not out.

It was such an impressive start that 'Old' Clarke quickly introduced him into the hallowed ranks of his touring All England Eleven. This came in 1846, in fact, soon after the Eleven was formed. Such a rapid rise to fame took the cricket public by storm, for he had actually played his first game at Lords as a 19 year old the year before, for the North against the M.C.C., just a week after his Notts debut. To play at Lords, for a player of that era, meant you had arrived.

He was a handsome man with large blue eyes and auburn hair, while a moustache and chin fringe set off his manly features nicely. Although of only average height, 5′ 9″, he weighed a solid 13 stones, and his rounded shoulders belied the fact that he was such a powerful stroke maker. The secret was in superb timing, with the initial help of

George Parr *right* with Notts Colleague Richard Daft
(Photograph dated 1862)

a stocky frame, and powerful fore-arms. Apart from a few basics suggested by William Clarke at the outset, he had received no tuition, and such a lack of know-how was obvious by his stance at the wicket. With his left knee bent, he crouched low over his bat held in a slanting position. Because his hands were inevitably too close to the ground, he received many nasty blows, with ensuing injuries to his fingers. From this seemingly uncomfortable position George Parr perfected shots all round the wicket, including hard square and late cuts, but surely it was leg side hitting that made him notorious, and to be dubbed 'Lion of the North'.

George Parr used little exertion, was diligent in defence, and severe off his back foot; quite unusual at that time. Because of his stance, he seemed tucked up when defending, but patience, and concentration, two attributes of W. G. Grace in later years, made him a prize scalp for all bowlers. Parr was considered the first batsman to play shots both sides of the wicket to straight balls. Many diehards held outspoken opinions that such tactics were detrimental to the game, but the effectiveness was plain for all to see. George Parr could steer balls through the leg side with an uncanny frequency, so much so that many of them must have been on the wicket. Using a sweep shot, or a drive of his legs, field placing became a nightmare for opposing captains. So many shots crashed into, and through, the branches of an elm tree on the leg side of Trent Bridge, that it became known as 'George Parr's tree'. His piratical batting methods raised many eyebrows in pavilion heirachies, as when Old Lillywhite denounced Parr's running out to drives as '. . . not cricket'. Alfred 'Ducky' Diver, the old Cambridge cricketer, was indignant when George Parr crashed a straight ball high over square leg. "Do you know where that ball pitched" the shocked bowler asked, halfway down the wicket. "In the hedge, I think!" Parr answered quietly.

Most bowling met the same fate, but Parr did prefer to bat against right arm bowling rather than left, as shown when Hinkley of Kent often took his wicket when the two counties met. On the batsman's own admission only the excessive speed of Harvey Fellowes singled him out as the only bowler that deprived the striker of such opportunities. To add to bowlers' frustrations, George Parr was an excellent judge of a quick single, which did nothing to temper desperate measures to keep him quiet.

Not surprisingly, many of 'Old' Clarke's idiosyncrasies surfaced in Parr's personality. His dislike of pre-match practice, together with a somewhat testy nature, often misinterpreted because of his shyness, were typical of the senior player's reactions on previous occasions. George Parr was also a strict skipper. With his temper on a short fuse, he would express himself to the point in no uncertain terms—but the players still thought the world of their captain. Young cricketers could always turn to him for advice, which he gave profusely, but, on the odd occasion, it was with tongue in cheek. Parr's general guide for a young aspirant was to present the umpire with a brace of birds, or rabbits, before the game, or comment on his father's cricketing ability, and perhaps a long innings would follow! Seasoned players also were recipients of his kindness and thoughtful consideration. Concerning more mundane happenings, George Parr could be very absent minded and forgetful, but the needs of his players were paramount. It was on his recommendation that Yorkshire took on George Freman, a fast bowler of high repute.

Upon the death of William Clarke in 1856, George Parr took over the reins of the All England Eleven, and totally abhorrant to his predecessor's opinions, matches were soon arranged with the rival United England Eleven. The cricketing public loved these battles, for it was watching the cream of the game in combat, a spectacle enjoyed all over the country. Three of his four centuries were made for the A.E.E. He saved his highest score of 130 for Notts against Surrey at the Oval, in 1859. It was the proudest day of his life when, at the end of his innings, an ecstatic crowd made a narrow alley for him to pass down from the wicket. His white straw hat in one hand, his bat in the other, his natural limp—a legacy of permanent rheumatism—took him to the pavilion gate, where £20 had been collected for him in a coconut shell. A nasty blow on the hand early in his innings made the knock more memorable. It was not unusual for Parr to be given monetary rewards by his doting public. Often at Lords and the Oval, he received such gifts to commemorate outstanding batting feats. In the first encounter between the two England elevens, in 1857, the players themselves made a collection for him in recognition of a splendid 56 not out in the first innings, and 19 not out in the second. He made 100 in his very first game for the A.E.E., which was against a Leicester XX, at Leicester, in 1847.

Parr performed many great deeds at the crease for the A.E.E., in accruing 10,404 runs, at an averaage of nearly 17—a good average on account of the rough wickets played on then. When the A.E.E. met the U.E.E. at Lords, in 1860, Parr hit a ball from William Caffyn, high over the Tavern. Caffyn explained how it was only slightly outside the leg stump, but that was enough, and it still finished in a garden on the other sie of St. John's Wood Road! Richard Daft, a Notts colleague and advocate, tended to Parr's A.E.E. match arrangements, and other correspondence; an administrative post taken on by William Oscroft in later years. George Parr received two benefit games, the first taking place at Lords, in 1858, between the two great England elevens. Although the weather was inclement, and the match finished in two days, a good crowd attended for both of them. His second match was when the North met the South at his beloved Trent Bridge, in 1878. Again, like 'Old' Clarke, Parr proved a businessman par excellence, making him a considerably wealthy person. It was every cricketer's ambition to play for either England Eleven. When writing to George Parr to recommend her son, E. M., for membership to the All England Eleven, Mrs. Grace made the point that she had a younger son at home who was going to be so much better, because his defence was so good!

George Parr's cricketing ability probably reflected the fact that his father, brothers and uncle had all been proficient performers. He was a good outfielder with an exceptional throwing arm from the boundary. On one occasion, at Lords, he won a £5 wager for Sir Frederick Bathurst in a cricket ball throwing contest with a soldier named Parkinson. His winning throw was measured at 108 yards 2 feet. In later years he concentrated on fielding in the slips area.

Trent Bridge, of course, was home to George Parr, but Lords, having played so many matches there, must have rated highly with him as a favourite ground. Many of his twenty-two games for the Players against the Gents took place there, between 1846 and 1865. Both dates had a significance, with the first being of a personal nature, while the second remains as one of cricket history's landmarks. On his debut, in 1846, he was bowled for a duck by Bathurst, and his last game, in 1865 was W. G. Grace's first as a sixteen year old. Parr was more successful in this encounter with 60 in the second innings. George Parr's 77 in the 1855 game at Lords was considered his greatest knock of this series, enabling the Players to win by seven wickets. He achieved a very high average of over 22 for the Players. Occasionally George Parr's underarm lob bowling was used to break up stubborn partnerships, but in the Oval encounter of 1859, he must have kept himself on, for he took 6 for 42, in an innings win for the Players—he made a little matter of 73 runs, as well!

George Parr's favourite pastime was obtained in the other sporting fields of shooting and angling. He loved nothing more than a day's snipe shooting by the Trent, with his constant companion, George Anderson, the noted Yorkshire cricketer. As on the cricket field, Parr's demeanour and sportsmanship towards his shooting friends was impeccable. If he thought there was a danger of taking a neighbour's shot, he would call "Your shot, sir". Although he loved to relax in the winter months around the fields and large estates, with his gun and dogs, if a business proposition presented itself, he was always interested. George Parr professed that he took up cricket because he disliked work, so when he and Johnny Wisden bought a cricket ground at Leamington, he must have wondered what he had let himself in for. "Farmer" George always bought their horses used in the rolling of the wickets, and as he objected to paying more than fifty shillings for them, they were a motley assortment. Wisden from Sussex, and Parr from Notts were both eligible to play some games for Warwickshire, because of the ground's location. Another business aspect of Parr's cricketing vocation was as Harrow's coach, where the pupils worshipped their illustrious tutor. It would appear that he taught them to practice by observation, as he spent many hours batting in the nets, with the students bowling to him!

North America received the very first touring party to leave these shores in 1859, and it was comprised of six players from the All England Eleven, and six from the United England Eleven. George Parr was automatically made skipper because of the high regard all his fellow players had for their popular leader. Alfred Shaw thought him the best skipper he had played under, while Richard Daft, a notable fellow Notts batsman, referred to him as "a man under whose banner I am proud to have fought, for a more honest and straightforward cricketer never took hold of a bat". Even such glowing accolades as these couldn't help him to cross the Atlantic—he proved a terrible sailor! It was an extremely powerful team that gave the far weaker opposition no chance. Cowering batsmen couldn't face the speed of John Jackson, while even George Parr took 16 wickets on the tour, with his slow underarms. Though successful, the team produced a few hiccups along the way. Parr had words with Frederick Lillywhite about the inconvenience created with the packing and travelling arrangement of the latter's printing machine and tent. Perhaps Parr had forgotten similar events concerning his indented hat box, inseparable from him when touring in England. How the young players tried to discover its contents, but to no avail! Parr had often worn high hats while playing, and was one of the last to wear the popular 'billycock' when others had discarded theirs.

The team was never in danger of losing a game, but some encounters did produce playing conditions 'foreign' to the tourists. Extreme cold caused the players to wear overcoats and gloves in some matches, and it was probably during one of these that Parr, having agreed to umpire, soon found a substitute, and retired to the pavilion for some gin and hot water!—his favourite beverage.

George Parr also captained the second tour of Australia and New Zealand, in 1863. Yet another strong party proved far superior, and returned unbeaten. Apart from two nasty bouts of erysipelas, Parr had to suffer his endemic fear of thunderstorms. He was known to hide down a cellar during a storm in England. A terror of sunstroke led him to acquire a special wide brimmed hat, with a curtain-like flap hanging from the back, to combat the severe heat. Such a nervous disposition was again tested when the tourists' boat was in collision with another, outside Sydney harbour.

Reaching New Zealand his shy, almost timid nature was again put under pressure. A Maori queen presented him with the highest honour possible, in the shape of an attractively woven mat to cover his shoulders, and made by members of her tribe. To Parr's utter chagrin, it was expected for the recipient to kiss the queen in traditional fashion. He tried to evade the issue by suggesting John Jackson perform the deed, as he was a 'gypsy'! George Parr eventually submitted, and when given a green stone by the royal lady, was told that if he carried it with him always, he would never work again—he did, and he didn't!

George Parr's popularity and deeds on the field of play helped to shape and influence cricket's future in many ways. He had been a wonderful ambassador abroad, and even had a hand in changing the laws of the game. When England met Kent at Canterbury in 1848, it was Alfred Mynn who had the honour of making the winning hit. Not to be outdone Parr ran and pocketed the ball. From then it was legislated that the ball is returned to the umpire, and not scrambled for by the 'outside'. It would appear this law was not strictly adhered to, as Pinder, at the end of Yorkshire's match with Notts at Bramall Lane, in 1878, had his collar-bone broken in the ensuing melee.

When Notts played a Nottinghamshire Gentlemen's XIV at Trent Bridge, in 1871, the game marked the end of Parr's playing career. Notts followers relished his two knocks of 32 not out and 53, and were proud to be present at the departure of their age-long leading star. Unlike other retired cricketers, George Parr was seldom seen at matches when his playing days ended, preferring to walk his two terriers, or gun dog. He became a sad looking figure, with a considerable loss of weight from his now quite bent frame, making him a shadow of his former self. Sadly, at the age of 65, and just eight months after marrying his house-keeper, Miss Smaley, George Parr died of rheumatic gout at his home at Radcliffe-on-Trent, in 1891.

On the day of his burial, Notts were playing Lancashire, at Trent Bridge, but the flag hung at half mast, and at burial time both teams stood with heads bowed as a mark of respect. George Parr was buried close to his great friend, Richard Daft, while the solitary wreath on the coffin was a branch from his Trench Bridge elm tree; his target just behind square leg.

CHAPTER FIVE

George Ulyett
(England & Yorkshire) 1851–1898

THE two ships officers eyed the embarking passengers with almost non-commital interest, until their attentions were attracted by a well built fellow struggling to the foot of the gang plank, carefully carrying a stone container. When questioned, he explained that he was to join Major R. Gardner Warton's touring cricketers in South Africa, as a replacement, and was asked to take out linseed oil as the fierce sun had dried out the cricket bats, causing them to crack and break. With the officers suitably convinced, George Ulyett stowed away the jar in his cabin, but not before tasting its contents, with a satisfied smile. A friend had kindly made him a parting gift of four gallons of whisky, probably in 'the true spirit of the game'!

Ulyett, one of cricket's earliest characters, was the Ian Botham of England from 1875 to 1890. He was born on October 21, 1851, at Pitsmoor, near Sheffield. A rule of the Pitsmoor Cricket Club restricted players under 18 from joining but, such was 16 year old Ulyett's potential after an initial refusal, that he became a member two months later. The rigorous daily life of a Sheffield steelwork's rolling mill helped to harden Ulyett's massive physique, and make his work easier. Many times he slipped away to play cricket but, with growing successes, such ability was impossible to keep secret. Each occasion was marked by the presentation of his dismissal notice, but he proved indispensible, was forgiven, and re-instated.

In 1871 Ulyett joined the Bradford club professionally. Near the end of a two year stay he played against the United South, at Bradford, and really brought his name to people's notice. With the United South wanting only 66 to win in their second innings, Ulyett bowled W. G. Grace for 34. This started a procession as Alan Hill and George Ulyett took six wickets without the batsmen crossing, and won the game for Bradford. This was Ulyett's first encounter with Grace—the "Big 'un", as he liked to refer to the doctor. Not surprisingly, Yorkshire signed him up after this match. Ulyett took

George Ulyett 1890

the field with the Yorkshire eleven for the first time in a game with Sussex, in 1873, at Bramall Lane, and played in the return at Brighton, a week later.

His London debut was scheduled when representing The North against The South at Prince's Ground, in 1875. Imagine his disappointment to learn that The North already had eleven players when he arrived, so W. G. Grace asked him to umpire instead. Was it with reluctance that Ulyett gave the "Big 'un" out L.B.W.

George Ulyett was a powerful man. Such a large frame is outstanding in old photographs and prints, like the base singer in a barber shop quartet, for his hair is parted in the middle, and a thick walrus moustache bristles from a cheery countenance. Tall and broad shouldered, he weighed 14 stones. Among his many virtues humour, perhaps, was paramount. His enjoyment of playing cricket was ever obvious, and he encouraged others to share it with him. Many stories illustrate his practical jokes, and Tom Emmett, a county colleague, predicted a stage career for him because he had the ability to carry out his pranks with a straight face. Perhaps Emmett was thinking of the occasion when Ulyett joined a procession of solemn faced schoolteachers, and marched with a serious expression. Sometimes he was on the receiving end when fellow players returned his harmless jests. When on tour once a telegram arrived in the dressing room for him, telling that his wife had given birth to twins. Typically, after the initial shock, he took it all in good part. It was Charles Ullathorne, a brilliant fielder in early Yorkshire elevens, who aptly named him "Happy Jack", because of his cheerfulness when things went badly for the team. To the faithful county supporters he was simply the original "Garge". George Hirst would become his successor.

Ulyett hit with immense power all round the wicket, including a drive over square leg, and his cutting was regal. He hit the ball out of Bramall Lane in 1883, while Sir Pelham Warner recalled how he smashed the bowling of W. Barnes over extra cover, into Block A, at Lords. The Lords pavilion was often a target but, after several direct strikes, he managed to miss it by going over the top. One day, when the genial Sammy Woods was in his fast bowling prime at Cambridge University, George Ulyett lofted him out of Fenners, and into a tub of mortar, being mixed to prepare footings for the houses in Woolaston Road. He once plundered 146 not out for Yorkshire against the M.C.C., at Scarborough, hitting the ball out of the ground three times. His logic in building a long innings was to hit the ball harder each time, this being the recommended method of defence.

George Ulyett's bowling was a match-winner seldom equalled. Although not able to control properly the swinging ball, his high action helped to achieve unsettling lift, and a sharp cut-back from the off. Sometimes movement in the air deserted him completely, while on other days, Lord Harris tells us, he needed a long-leg to counteract his wide swerving deliveries. For such a composed character. Ulyett had a superstitious tendency, because if he missed his run-up early in the game, it was proof he would not take a wicket that day, and would ask to be taken off. When batting he only took guard once.

Luckily, this quirk of human nature did little to affect his performance, because he soon became one of Yorkshire's king-pins. He opened the batting and bowling for a period, and captained the side in the absence of Lord Hawke. The latter turned to Ulyett as his senior professional, but John Tunnicliffe took over his role later. The importance of George Ulyett's presence in the Yorkshire eleven is described in Wisden 1882, when stating that if he had been available for the three games he missed, Yorkshire would probably have won the title in 1881. Apart from the occasional glass of beer, Ulyett thrived on hard fought tussles, games of cut and thrust, when players battled to narrow wins. The Roses clashes served to appease his appetite. In the Sheffield game, 1883, he did the hat trick and scored 61, an exhibition that gave him immense pleasure. Even in such strained situations Ulyett introduced a smile, as when taking a position of close point to Lancashire batsman, Richard Barlow. Taking guard Barlow muttered to Ulyett, "Get back, Jack, I wouldn't like to kill thee". As Barlow was never recognised as a hard hitter, point laughingly replied "If tha did, Dick, I'd be t'first tha'd killed with hard hitting!" A few balls later the luckless batsman cut a loose ball outside the off stump, only to see Ulyett, effortlessly, pluck the ball out of the air.

George Ulyett's opening partner was Louis Hall, a product of the Yorkshire nursery at Lascelles Hall. It is difficult to imagine two such opposites, for Hall was a Methodist preacher, and a total abstainer. The pair were referred to as 'the saint' and 'the sinner', while Yorkshire wits suggested that when Louis played the organ, George played the fool! The two were first on the list of great opening partnerships Yorkshire contributed to cricket. Eleven times Hall and Ulyett produced opening century stands and, in 1885, they accomplished it in each innings, against Sussex. In a remarkable game at Canterbury in 1887, Yorkshire's first three batsmen each reached a century, with Ulyett's 124 made out of the first 169 runs. Between 1873 and 1893 he played 407 games for the county, scoring over 16,000 runs, averaging 24. In five seasons he made over 1,000 runs, and of his 18 centuries, 15 were for Yorkshire. He took nearly 500 wickets, averaging 18. It would have been a mighty task getting Ulyett to quote these statistics, as modesty was yet another of his virtues. When A. W. Pullin—alias "Old Ebor"—was compiling notes for his book 'Talks with Old English Cricketers', it was essential that he interviewed George Ulyett. Many appointments were cancelled at the last minute because Ulyett had received a telegram or postcard, calling him away. These excuses were finally thwarted by the author asking a friend of Ulyett to call on the cricketer, and Pullin accompanied him. George Ulyett was far too modest to discuss his many successes.

To be chosen for the Gents v Players game at Lords was, at this period of cricket's history, the acme of any cricketer's career. Even after the first Test Match of 1877, the honour of representing either the Gentlemen or the Players was for several decades more prestigious than gaining England selection. George Ulyett played his first game for the Players, albeit at the Oval, in 1875, but fulfilled an ambition the following year, at Lords. Between 1875 and 1892 he starred 37 times, with many feats of wicket-taking and consistently high scores with the bat. In 65 innings he made nearly 1,800 runs, with an average of 27, and his 30 wickets cost 30 runs each. the highlights started with 53 and 118 at Prince's in 1877, while in 1881, at The Oval, he opened the batting with 57 and 80. At Lords, in 1883, scores of 65 and 51 established him as a firm favourite with the public. The following year he hit 134 out of 213 while at the wicket. This Oval slaughter was just the prelude to his 96 and 64 at Lords, a few days later. This popular fixture, over the years, is studded with Ulyett's all-round performances.

The first Test Match between Australia and England was arranged to be played at Melbourne, over four days, and Ulyett represented England in this great milestone. Although achieving little success, he was able to make amends in the second Test, two weeks later, with scores of 52 and 63, helping England to a 4 wicket victory, thus avenging Australia's win in the previous game. This touring team of professionals was managed, and captained, by James Lillywhite, and Ulyett had every cause to be satisfied with his showing, thus making future selection almost a formality.

Lord Harris skippered the next England tourists in 1878–9, a team composed of twelve amateurs, plus two Yorkshire professionals, Tom Emmett and George Ulyett. Even though the results were not good, Ulyett proved the main run-getter, and topped the batting averages. Sadly, this tour will be remembered for the unsavoury scenes at Sydney, when Murdoch, the New South Wales captain, was adjudged run out. This action caused onlookers to encroach upon the playing

area where, after being attacked, Lord Harris was escorted safely to the
pavilion by his two pro's, each wielding a stump. George Ulyett certainly had more pleasant memories, for he had taken four wickets in
four balls. Batting with his captain, Ulyett was instructed to take things
easy, and build a good score. His response was to hit at almost every
ball, together with an apology that "he felt he had a hitting fit on." To
Yorkshire supporters this action recalled a similar situation during a
Roses match, when Yorkshire wanted six runs to win with just the last
wicket standing. Ulyett tried to hit Johnny Briggs out of the ground,
and was caught on the boundary. There were no recriminations, or
harsh words, when discussing the narrow Lancashire win, because it was
accepted that that was the way Ulyett played his cricket.

Alfred Shaw led the 1881-2 team that travelled to New Zealand
and Australia, via America. Playing a game in San Francisco, a
baseball pitcher was chosen by the opposition to baffle the crack
batsmen with his ability to make the ball dip and swerve in flight.
After Ulyett had thrashed 167 not out in a short time, the dejected
pitcher openly showed his disgust with the game of cricket! In the
first class games of that tour, Ulyett scored the only century, with a
classic 149 in the third Test Match, at Melbourne. His highest score
ever was 199 not out made against Derbyshire, in 1887. Twice more
he travelled to Australia and, of course, to South Africa in 1888-9.
When J. H. Roberts was allowed to return, because of a family
bereavement, Ulyett joined the first party ever to tour South Africa.
Sir Aubrey C. Smith captained this successful side, and must have
been delighted to receive such a potent bat liniment.

Of George Ulyett's home Tests, the Oval game of 1882 was his
bitterest memory. The mythical Ashes were born when Australia beat
England by 7 runs, after the home team failed to get the 87 runs
needed for victory in the second innings. Ulyett thought the English
batsmen allowed themselves to be intimidated by the speed of the
Spofforth, after all ". . . me and the Doctor had made half of 'em",
he lamented. He often explained that his England selection was based
on his talent for whistling and, possibly, for good behaviour! He had
more pleasant memories of the Lords Test in 1884, but, probably,
more painful. George Bonnor, batting at number six for Australia,
and an even bigger man Ulyett at 16 stones and 6' 6" tall, crashed a
half-volley back towards the bowler. All eyes followed the ball's
imaginary line of flight to the boundary, but Ulyett had caught it in
his follow through, much to the horror of many eye-witnesses. Lord
Harris and W. G. Grace said he was silly to try for it, and "Punch"
magazine proposed that he could be useful catching cannonballs in
wartime! After Ulyett finished with 7 for 36, from 39 overs and 23

maidens, England won by an innings and 5 runs, and Ulyett was presented with the ball. Mr. Grimston, an ageing Lords member, and respected critic, gave the hero of the hour a gold coin to commemorate the finest catch he had ever seen. In the first Test at Manchester, 1886, George Ulyett was batting when the scores were level. His vast hit into the outfield heralded a stampede by watching reporters to describe England's 5 wicket victory to their waiting editors. He, unintentionally, had the last laugh again, when Garrett caught him on the boundary. This, eventual, 4 wicket win was set up with Ulyett's 4 for 46 in Australia's first innings. He played his last test Match in 1890, at Lords of all places. It was a fitting stage from which to take his final curtain-call, and he did it in style. England only made a meagre 173 in the first innings, but Ulyett contributed 74 most valuable runs. His innings set the foundation for a victory for England by 7 wickets. In 23 Tests he made nearly 1,000 runs, and took 50 wickets. He was the first English batsman to score a Test century, and 50 runs in each innings of a Test Match.

In recognition of loyal and outstanding service to his county, Yorkshire arranged a benefit match for George Ulyett against Surrey, in 1887, the Jubilee Year of Queen Victoria. Unfortunately, the game was finished in two days, but disappointing gate receipts were enhanced by £700, from a subscription list. The final figure was a pleasing one of four digits. After retiring from cricket in 1893, Ulyett became a publican for a short period. Through cricket he had been left in reasonably comfortable circumstances, due mainly, to his own explanation "being lucky in getting so many trips across the water".

His home ground of Bramall Lane had always been his favourite to play on, but now he liked nothing better than to sit and watch his beloved Yorkshire, so successful, and still under the leadership of Lord Hawke. On one bitterly cold June day in 1898, Ulyett met George Hirst on the pavilion steps and, putting his hand on Hirst's shoulder, slowly confided "Young 'Un"—he always called George Hirst by this name, "I'm finished". He caught pneumonia and died before the end of that week. Such a sad prediction had been fulfilled, just a mile or two from his birth place, and at the tragically young age of 47. There have been many English cricketing heroes since; perhaps they were fortunate to be set such an outstanding example, by one of the first.

CHAPTER SIX

John 'Foghorn' Jackson (Notts C.C.) 1833–1901

ON the 21st May 1833 John Jackson was born in Bungay, Suffolk but within a week the Jackson family moved home to Nottingham. As a lad John ran with the hounds in Retford country ". . . wearing a red coat and leading terriers . . ."; often barefoot. Forsaking the usual targets of windows and birds, John Jackson chose to aim his stones at signposts and milestones—direct hits were often scored using his natural bowling action. About this period he answered to the nickname of 'Jem Crow'.

Jem's early cricket practice was taken at the Southwell ground where he was paid 6d. an hour to field and bowl, after which he had a seven mile walk home. It was during these practices that William Clarke recognised the high quality of performance and offered him a game with the Notts XI in 1855.

Weighing 14 stones—increasing later to 15 stones—and standing 6′ he was superbly proportioned. With an easy shoulder-level action John bowled well within himself, but was still able to produce great speed, sustained for long sessions. The ball tended to move with the arm and it was acclaimed that his right-arm expresses, ". . . were suited to all weathers . . ." This pace was generated from a short run of 4 or 5 yards and was scrupulously fair at all times.

George Parr, the popular Notts captain, was presented with many tricky situations due to John's rough and ready character. Once, when touring in Cornwall, the team stopped at a farm for refreshments. John Jackson quickly disappeared into the dairy only to emerge later with a tell-tale 'beard' of clotted cream around his chin—the rest of the team had to go without. His swarthy, lightly bearded features almost confirmed the story that more than just a spot of Romany blood was present. His looks were not improved by an accident while playing in the nets at Cambridge where he was struck on the nose by the ball. Some kindly person brought a quantity of rum to rub on the injury, but John drank the 'embrocation'

John 'Foghorn' Jackson

and went to the pavilion for some hot water. After this setback his nose always appeared to be slipping to one side.

The year 1855 saw John Jackson playing his first game for the celebrated All England Eleven and it was in such company that his class finally blossomed. During his short career Jackson had fast bowling partners in Tarrant, Grundy and Willsher, also the slow underarm spinner Tinley. In one game, with John's expresses in partnership with 'tweakers' from Tinley, a despondent gentleman, upon reaching the pavilion after a quick dismissal, was heard to say, "what chance does a man stand with a thunderbolt at one end and a corkscrew at the other?". John batted 412 times in 252 matches for the All England Eleven totalling 2,714 runs and taking 2,187 wickets.

On the June 30, 1856 John played his first game at Lords for the North v South, but he was used sparingly, only taking 3 wickets and scoring 0 and 12. After this quiet opening he started to create havoc against the teams of Twenty-Two and Eighteen, so popular in this era. Startling wicket-taking feats emerged as these less skilful batsmen took evasive action to retain life and limbs. It was about this time that Robert Carpenter, the renowned Cambridge batsman christened John 'Foghorn', because each time he took a wicket the event was recorded by him blowing his nose deafeningly.

Jackson was no mean performer with the bat; being more from the bludgeoning mould than the classical, he used his long reach effectively, hitting powerfully forward and to the leg. Among many useful contributions was a good 100 for Notts v Kent at Cranbrook in 1863—in the same match he took 12 wickets for 43 runs and caught 3 batsmen off Grundy's bowling. John would not take payment in bank notes—only gold, and when batting for Notts one day his trousers split, causing gold coins to spill over the wicket. In a rich Notts brouge he instructed everyone to stand well clear, while he retrieved his money personally!

John Jackson's stamina was never questioned, for on no less than five occasions he bowled unchanged through an innings—this included Gents v Players at Lords in 1861 when he and Willsher bowled unchanged through both innings, with Jackson taking 11 for 99. John played 12 times for the Players being on the winning side 11 times with 1 drawn: this winning monopoly was then broken with the arrival of Dr. W. G. Grace. When the North played the South at Canterbury in 1859, Jackson and Grundy dominated proceedings by bowling unchanged with the former taking 12–74; in that year the Canterbury wicket was considered easy paced. Later that year he had the distinction of being selected for the first American Tour, where he took many wickets, but he proved to be a poor sailor.

Hostility was a part of John Jackson's make-up that many cricketers were made painfully aware of, for batting must have been a nightmare on the notoriously rough wickets of this period. William Caffyn, in his book '71 Not Out', admits that there were occasions when even he was not sorry to be out, and back in the safety of the pavilion. John's regular destruction of the XXII's and XVIII's gained him yet another name—'the Demon', and the energy he expended on these inferior teams no doubt shortened his first class playing career to just 11 years. 'The Demon', like most bowlers, hated the isolated punishing innings, such as when that illustrious hitter C. I. Thornton put the ball into an adjoining field twice off sucessive deliveries. John hitched his trousers and growled "Oh, to Hell with that kind of batting". When a batsman had the audacity to hit him that hard, Jackson's next ball would be bowled waist high, at terrific speed, only to pitch on to the metal stump tops. On other numerous occasions the ball seemed to slip and pass uncomfortably close to the batsman's head!

John Jackson was the first cricketer to enter the pages of 'Punch', with a cartoon depicting a well bandaged batsman having just faced an over from him. Jemmy Grundy, in the England v United England game of 1861, was struck such a blow that ". . . he stamped and swore like a lunatic . . ." Another poor unfortunate was hit on the ankle and promptly limped away, but when it was made clear that he was not out, he retorted "No, but I'm going". When 'Old Ebor' was compiling his book 'Old English Cricketers', he interviewed John Jackson, who recalled ". . . I never got all 10 wickets but I once did something as good. It was in the North v the South match at Nottingham. I got 9 wickets and lamed Johnny Wisden so that he could not bat. That was as good as 10, eh? . . ."

'The Demon's' ferocity was perfectly summed up when Prowse wrote his elegy to Alfred Mynn with the opening words "Jackson's pace is very fearful". Apart from pace, John's other asset was accuracy, as the game between the All England Eleven and XXII of Uppingham demonstrated, when he hit the stumps 6 times in 7 balls. From 1856 to 1862 he captured the staggering number of 1899 wickets, including an average bag of 345 for 3 consecutive years. A challenge match between the three 'kings' of Cambridge, namely Hayward, Tarrant and Carpenter, and three from Nottingham, consisting of Jackson, Daft and Clarke, was played at Trent Bridge on the 4th July, 1862. After big John had dismissed all three for just one run, the Notts trio won easily. Renowned batsmen, such as R. D. Walker and W. Caffyn, considered him to be the most difficult fast bowler to face in their day. The year 1863 saw John Jackson as a member of the 2nd Australian touring party under the leadership of George Parr. John underlined his greatness as a cricketer, but was still one of the worst sailors.

During the Notts v Yorkshire game of 1866, John Jackson took a heavy fall when running to retrieve a ball, while fielding. In great pain it was found he had broken a blood vessel behind the knee, causing him to be out of action for 20 weeks. Sadly, his playing days for Notts C.C. were terminated at the age of 33! When talking to 'Old Ebor', John suggested he was dropped because of not actually being born in the County.

After his Notts commitments he played for Burnley, Liverpool and in Ireland, with Liverpool, in 1871, engaging John as caterer, groundsman and bowler. For past services a benefit game was played at Trent Bridge in 1874 for 'Old Jack', as he was affectionately known in his latter days, and he was presented with the princely sum of £262. 2s. 6d.

From the dizzy heights of a story-book playing career he sunk to the depths of a down and out, ending his working days as a bent, grey bearded warehouseman, in Liverpool. With many kindnesses from his friends in the North, 'Old Jack's' weekly budget was enhanced by 6/- from the Cricketers' Fund Friendly Society.

So, in November 1901 at the age of 68, John Jackson passed away in the Liverpool Workhouse Infirmary, but these same loyal friends saved him from the indignity of a pauper's grave.

CHAPTER SEVEN

George Lohmann
(Surrey & England) 1865–1901

In the warm morning sunshine the Surrey Colts were enjoying their
pre-match net practice, and George was eagerly bowling to his friend
who was to play in the game starting shortly. After a few overs
George was granted the courtesy to bat, and, even though concen-
trating on the job in hand, he could not help but wonder that he was
actually using the same nets that current Surrey stars, W. W. Read
and A. P. Lucas batted in for their practice. This reverie was shattered when John Newton, the head groundsman at the Oval, ordered
him gruffly out of the net as he was not playing in the match, and
had no right to be there. Despondently, the lad did as he was told,
but other eyes had been watching—eyes that recognised outstanding
ability in one so young.

Walking away he was met by Dick Humphrey, a prominent Surrey
player of the seventies, who asked if it was he who had just been
batting. Tentatively, George replied that it was, and, as if he was
dreaming, he heard the old professional say "Will you bat again as
the Hon. Robert Grimston would like to have another look at you?"
This gentleman was the pioneer of the Surrey Colts and net practice
for young potentials. He was astounded at the lad's technique to hit
the ball fluently, and his variation of length and pace when bowling.
C. W. Alcock was quietly amused to see this stocky lad rub the ball
in the dust and wet his fingers before bowling: tricks used by seasoned professionals. The watching Surrey committee members had no
hesitation in asking George to play in the first Colts match the
following season in April 1884. After a successful debut he accepted
the invitation to join the full Surrey staff, and played for the County
XI within a month, at the age of 19.

George Lohmann was born at Kensington on the 2nd June 1865.
Leaving school in 1879 he grafted for two years to earn a living, and
played his early cricket on Wandsworth Common for the Church
Institute Club. For three successive years from 1876 he won the

39

George Lohmann

Club's prizes of cricket bats and balls for heading both the batting and bowling averages. In 1881 George moved on to the Alma Club. George Lohmann was actually qualified to play for three Counties, for he had been born in Middlesex, resided in Hampshire, and his father had lived in Surrey. As a lad George saved his pennies to watch his idols at the Oval, and when the offer came along to join the Surrey staff he jumped at it. His first season with Surrey proved rather quiet with few bowling chances, but he batted with much promise. Around the middle of the season he was dropped from the side, but soon returned, and in the last match against Sussex he took nine wickets for 58 runs enabling Surrey to win.

George had now "arrived" on the cricket scene and would become the finest all-rounder ever to play for Surrey. He was always in the game by making quick runs particularly when wanted, and taking half chances when offered to second slip, or cover-slip as it was then known. He virtually created this new position and was to become the game's number one exponent of it. W. G. Grace remarked how he covered more ground at slip than anyone he could remember, but towards the end of a rather short career George would fall full length to stop the easy ones. Sir Pelham Warner thought him good enough to be able to show off like this in front of his many fans. When George first played cricket he wasn't particularly bothered about fielding until he noticed how good the keenest cricketers were. He was unsurpassed at second slip and cricket followers marvelled at his cat-like movements, but cricket, being the great leveller it is, found him wanting on one occasion when he was brought on as a substitute in a Gents v Players match at Scarborough. Immediately being put in his specialist position at slip he dropped a 'sitter' off the first ball.

It was as a bowler cricket enthusiasts flocked to see him, whenever possible. This good looking, splendidly built athlete moved with the utmost ease, and caused all sorts of problems for the leading Test batsmen of this era. Standing 5' 11" and weighing 12 stones 12 pounds his fair, wavy hair accentuated his Anglo-Saxon features. With a high, graceful action he bowled right arm medium pace from either round or over the wicket. He used such variation in length and pace that he never seemed to bowl two balls alike. His stock ball was the off-cutter, but often he would mix in a leg-cutter, or the dangerous one that kept straight on. George was a great example of practice making perfect, and always carried a cricket ball in his pocket to wrap his fingers round to spin and manipulate.

In 1885 he was chosen to play in the North v the South game at the Oval, and in the summer of 1886 he made his Test debut against the visiting Australians. So in less than two seasons he had graduated from Club to Test cricket. In the first two Tests he had little success, but when bowling on his home pitch at the Oval in the third match, he was unplayable. Having match figures of 12 for 104 he enabled England to win by an innings and 217 runs. In the winter of '86 he toured Australia under the leadership of Shaw and Shrewbury. It wasn't long before the Australian press was giving superb write-ups about his prowess, attributed to guile and hard work. It was a clear case of him being overbowled, because, after countless overs, he took 153 wickets on the tour. Only two Tests were played, with England winning both, and in the first innings of the second Test George Lohmann took 8 for 35—he was leading wicket taker in the Test matches with 16.

The year 1887 was a good one for George with the bat. After useful knocks for Surrey, he ended the season with an average of 28.9 runs. He was off to Australia again that winter in a team managed by Arthur Shrewsbury and skippered by C. Aubrey-Smith. Another team from England was touring down-under at the same time, and a side was selected from the two parties to play a Test Match at Sydney on Februay 10th. England won by 126 runs with Peel and Lohmann taking nine wickets each.

Most critics assessed 1888 as George's peak year, because apart from batting well he bowled with tremendous zest and stamina. With the Australians here again England's run of seven Test wins was broken when Australia took the Lords game by 61 runs—England winning the next two Tests. The Oval Test saw George snap up two miraculous catches in the first innings to dismiss both Australian openers Bannerman and McDonnell: the former talked about little else for the rest of the day. England built a useful lead after George had scored an impressive and unbeaten 62, and won by an innings. That season he took a record 45 catches. At Manchester, England won the game quite easily in a day and a half so George, typically in character, agreed to play for a local side on the Saturday. On a terrible wicket he bowled with his usual skill until the local rival fast bowler started to hit him to all parts of the ground. Everything the batsman tried was successful and George, for once in his career, was taken apart. Eager for revenge George batted early in the order but was bowled first ball by his rival and, with the bowler boasting loudly of his accomplishment, the Surrey star quickly packed his bag and departed. The crowd voiced its opinion that he must have been a fraud—it wasn't the real George Lohmann.

During the '80's and '90's W. G. Grace and George Lohmann were recognised as the greatest match winners in the game. Surrey shared a triple tie for the Championship in 1889 due mainly to a great victory over Nottinghamshire in August. This was the year of the new declaration law and John Shuter, the Surrey captain, risked a quick closure, hoping George could oblige with quick wickets. After 35 overs, including 26 maidens, he took 6 for 22, and Notts were all out for 84 with 40 minutes to go. When Surrey played Essex earlier, George scored 105 and, with Sharpe, put on 149 for the last wicket.

Australia visited us again in 1890 and three Tests were to be played. One was abandoned because of bad weather, but England won the remaining two, with George taking 9 wickets. This summer he broke his own record with 49 catches. It was generally agreed that Australia's batting had not been particularly strong over the last few years, but this did not detract anything from George's wonderful achievements, for he was producing the same results against our own top class batsmen in County and representative games. C. B. Fry reckoned George Lohmann to be the most difficult medium paced bowler he ever played against on a good wicket. That great scholar and athlete was heard to say ". . . it took an absolutely first rate batsman to know what an honour it was to be bowled at by Lohmann". W. G. Grace rated him as the best all rounder he encountered during his 35 years of first class cricket.

For most years George had average about 20 with the bat, but in 1891 he raised it to 23. The winter of 1891–2 saw him leaving for Australia, again under the leadership of W. G. Grace. George was the power-house of a very strong party, but still Australia ran out winners by two Tests to one. In the first innings of the second Test he helped bowl out the opposition for 144, taking 8 for 58, but with England collapsing in their second innings, Australia still managed victory by 72 runs. On five occasions during his career George Lohmann bowled unchanged through an innings, and his appetite for bowling was nicely illustrated on this tour when, W.G. suggested he should change the bowling at George's end. The bowler agreed and immediately set his field to bowl from the other end! The Doctor, in retrospect, pointed out that it was not done in selfishness, but because he was so keen, and knew his own ability to take a wicket at any time. To bowl on good, Australian wickets George maintained that the secret was variation of pace and thoughtful field placing, and the fact that his Surrey colleague, Tom Richardson, could move the ball off the wickets made him, in George's opinion, the 'King' in such conditions.

George Lohmann was a cricketer's cricketer. His fellow players held him in great esteem for he was a perfectionist in his art. Every movement, whether batting, bowling or fielding was made with consummate ease, and in George's eyes that was the only way to play the game. It was said he helped to make cricket an attractive game to watch. Albert Knight, the old Leicester professional, recalls the day when George was bowled neck and crop by a young bowler using intimidating methods. Passing the grinning victor, George surveyed him in utter disdain, and said in a cutting tone "Call that bowling? I call it brute strength".

It was obvious in 1892 that George was less effective, and this was attributed to so many summers and winters of continuous hard work. With such a willing workhorse it was inevitable that he would be over bowled. It was thought that a winter's rest would re-vitalise him—he was now 27 years old—but unfortunately this was not to be, because soon. after the season's end he collapsed. Through the generosity of the Surrey County Cricket Club he, together with his great friend Maurice Read for company, sailed from Southampton on Christmas Eve for South Africa, where he stayed in the Ceres Sanitorium, 90 miles from Cape Town. To recuperate George, and Maurice, were invited to the home of cricket enthusiast J. D. Logan, which was ideally situated high in the mountains at Matjesfontein, the air being dry and crystal clear. With George having made such good progress and seeming to be so much better, Maurice Read returned to England in mid March to prepare for the start of the English season. Hopes were raised when a friend received a letter from George saying that his weight had returned to 12 stones, and he was taking daily cricket practice. About mid-June he landed at Southampton, but, in trying to get back too soon, sadly he had a relapse. Again through arrangements by Surrey, he returned to Mr. Logan's home in the Orange Free State, and stayed for the rest of 1893 and 1894.

In the late '80's Surrey were a good side but, with George Lohmann quickly reaching his prime, the side sparked to greatness. J. Shuter, the successful Surrey skipper, rated him the greatest cricketer of his time. When George stopped playing in 1893, Surrey dropped from top to fifth in the table. His absence from the cricket field was telling, but England hopes were lifted when, in 1895, a letter from him told of his being on the way to complete recovery. He had recently played for the Cape Town club in a two day fixture, and had taken 8 for 70 with no ill effects. Leaving Cape Town on the 8th June George was practising at Lords just three weeks after this last game.

George Lohmann played in the Gents v Players game at the Oval on July 11th and, although not outstanding, his form was encouraging. With Lockwood out of form, George partnered Tom Richardson to produce Surrey's spearhead, and their success was measured in the first averagesm with Tom in first position and George third. A letter from George to William Attewell before the end of the season suggested, however, that he was not as fit as at first thought.

In the winter of 1895–6, Lord Hawke took George Lohmann to South Africa as player manager of his touring team, and what a tour the latter had. England beat South Africa in all three Tests, due almost certainly to George taking 35 wickets at 3.8 runs each, including the hat trick. In the last Test he passed 100 wickets in only his 16th Test Match, and that remains a record. Against an XVIII at Port Elizabeth George bowled unchanged to take 15 for 38 and 11 for 44 in the match. In all games he took 157 wickets. Sir Pelham Warner was a young member of the party and recalls with pleasure his many enjoyable chats with George. 'Plum' tells of George's intelligent conversation and nice manners, and how he saved his pocket money as a youngster to watch George play at the Oval. He remembered the occasion when he saw George and Maurice Read each make 66 runs on a sticky Oval wicket against the might of Lancashire, with Barlow, Briggs and Mold at their best.

The Australians, under Harry Trott, visited us in 1896, and when Tom Richardson and George bowled them out for 53 in the first Test at Lords, England won comfortably by six wickets. With Australia winning the Second Test by the margin of three wickets the teams went to the Oval all square. When the England team was announced five of the professionals went on 'strike', demanding £20 as opposed to £10 normally paid for Test matches. The 'strikers' were Bobby Abel, Tom Richardson, Tom Haywood, George Lohmann—all of Surrey—and Billy Gunn of Notts. The Surrey Club refused the demands although it was considered that the principal was right, but the method ill-advised. After discussions Abel, Haywood and Richardson withdrew their requests and played, but, although George apologised, it was too late for him to take part. England won the Test by 66 runs. George's action reflected badly as he had just received a benefit in the game with Yorkshire, which brought him a larger pavilion subscription list than any other Surrey player had ever received before. He wrote a touching letter, and Surrey selected him for the rest of the games that season. Although taking 93 wickets and averaging 22 with the bat, his critics remained unhappy about his performance.

At the end of the 1896 season he returned to South Africa, but intended to come back in time to practice for the coming season with Surrey: it was announced in December that he had booked his passage. Regrettably, this was not the case as he had accepted a winter business position, and was playing as an amateur for Western Province in the Currie Cup. Needless to add, they won the competition with George taking 34 wickets at 12.26 runs each. In the final, Western Province triumphed over Transvaal and he had match figures of 10 for 157.

April 1897 brought another confrontation between George Lohmann and Surrey, for he wanted to play here in the summer and go back to South Africa for the winter. He asked Surrey for £100 to cover the travelling, but they offered to pay only half his expenses. George refused this gesture and it was announced on May 6th that he had terminated his association with the Club. Sadly, this was the end of his competitive cricket. He had played in 18 Tests, and had taken 10 or more wickets five times, including a hat trick. His 112 wickets at 10.75 runs each in so few Tests is still unique. From 1884 to 1896 he took 1805 wickets in first class cricket at 13.91 runs, and scored 7,348 runs for an average of 18.92.

George Lohmann took a keen interest in South African cricket and was a coach with the Wanderers Club in Johannesburg. He was enthusiasitc and quite gifted at spotting young talent—perhaps he was often reminded of that warm sunny morning at the Oval nets. In 1901 George came to England as manager of the touring South Africans but, for his old acquaintances, he was a pitiful sight as he had deteriorated so much. Still only 36 years old, and still a bachelor, he returned home to South Africa, where, on December 1st, he tragically died from consumption. In the Matjesfontein Cemetery an impressive headstone carried this inscription:-

GEORGE ALFRED LOHMANN
Born June 2nd 1865
Died December 1st 1901

"This monument was erected by the Surrey County Cricket Club and friend in South Africa in memory of one of the greatest all round cricketers the world has ever seen. A bowler of infinite variety, a spendid field, and a resolute batsman. He did brillian service for Surrey from 1884–1896, as well as for the Players and for England. His whole heart was in cricket, and he played the game from start to finish. Ill health alone compelled him to retire from the cricket field while still in his prime."

CHAPTER EIGHT

Johnny Briggs
(England & Lancashire) 1862 – 1902

IF it were possible to organise a poll to discover the player who had given Lancashire's legions of supporters the most entertainment over the club's past one hundred and twenty three years of cricket, the name of Johnny Briggs would be very near the top. Although he was born at Sutton-in-Ashfield, Nottinghamshire on October 3rd, 1862, the Old Trafford crowds took him to their hearts immediately for his boyish humour and looks, not to mention the bouncy movements when bowling and fielding. After the family moved to Lancashire when Johnny Briggs was a mere tot, he soon found the friendly environment much to his liking and the adoption of a new county no hardship.

It was a fateful day in 1878 when those two old Lancashire professionals, Richard Barlow and Alec Watson, played in a benefit game at Liverpool. The enthusiasm shown by a fourteen year old lad caused both veterans to recommend him immediately to the Lancashire Committee for a trial, which duly occurred that same year. The youngster, Johnny Briggs, went to live with Richard Barlow, who, with Alec Watson, coached the talented youth in all aspects of the game. Such lodgings and sound advice lasted for two years, during which time Johnny played five times for the county in 1879, but he found the going tough, especially when the fans thought a joke had been played on them, when seeing such a youthful person taking the field for the first time! Although Lancashire persevered, it was not until 1883 that Johnny's batting showed signs of improving to county standards. It was as a fast-medium left arm bowler that Briggs only took nine wickets in his first six years, but by reducing his pace, wickets and success came his way from 1885. This rise in achievement was a blessing to Lancashire, for it coincided with the exit from county cricket of Crossland, because of a suspect bowling action, together with a qualification irregularity when he lived in Nottinghamshire for a few months—quite ironic really, when considering Briggs' birthplace.

Johnny Briggs

Johnny Briggs' lovable nature endeared him to all his fellow players, and the crowds, no matter if at home or away, seemed to find his love of cricket, and life in general, contagious. Children were enchanted by him, for he often stopped to join their games in the streets on his way home from Old Trafford, after play had ended in the current county game. They loved his keenness when stopping a hard hit shot from an urchin's make-shift cricket bat. They noticed how his blue bulbous eyes sparkled from a widish face, while a snub nose and broad smiling mouth gave him a friendly toad-like expression. It was not surprising that such a dashing personality was accident-prone, but sometimes close associates would notice how his mouth would droop at the corners and his eyes stare unseeing in a pathetic trance for just a moment. Perhaps these were signs of the inner turmoil he suffered silently, for he lived under the permanent threat of epilepsy.

Probably to describe his batting style as mercurial is slightly inadequate, so much so when reading Neville Cardus' more musical description of a typical Johnny Briggs innings as ". . . racing along like a scherzo". Johnny Briggs stood only 5' 8" tall, and it was a mystery where he found such power and sustained aggression from his almost portly frame. Batting right handed, and quite low in the order, he loved to slash an off-side ball on the up, between cover and third man, the ball often clearing the latter's surprised upward gaze! Using his well worn, and much bound bat, he was capable of makng 50 at any time. Indeed his highest innings was 186 against Surrey at Liverpool, in 1885. This was made possible when Richard Pilling stayed with him in a last wicket stand of 173, which is still a county record, but the fact that it was achieved the day after Johnny's wedding makes it that bit more remarkable! His captain, 'Monkey' Hornby, suggested he got married more often if it had that effect on him! In first class cricket his total of nearly 14,000 runs (10,600 for Lancashire), included nine centuries.

Of Johnny Briggs' fielding at cover-point, it was thought there was little difference between him and the other Lancashire expert, Vernon Royle—praise indeed! The former's speed in picking up and returning never diminished, his joints seemingly elasticated, especially when fielding to his own bowling, when he needed no mid-on or mid-off.

If Johnny Briggs caught the imagination of the Lancashire faithfuls when batting and fielding, their hearts raced and blood pressures soared when he took the ball. Taking only three or four walking paces to the wicket his ever present disarming smile seemed to compensate for the hidden wiles of his well flighted left arm deliveries. When not using a deceptively faster ball, his immense finger spin clicked audibly as far as the pavilion. He bowled his overs in rapid time, giving the poor batsmen no respite from the constant taunting pressure of deciding which way the ball would turn. Briggs would sometimes alter his strategy on a good wicket by throwing up the ball to tempt a batsman, and even if it proved a little more expensive, his ploys generally worked out. Another of his many options was to bowl from two yards behind the delivery line, and how well C.B. Fry summed up Johnny's expertise as ". . . a professor of diddling, considered as one of the exact sciences!"

Many of Lancashire's successes were mainly due to Johnny Briggs' left arm. In 1885 he headed the county's bowling averages with 79 wickets costing just 10.5 runs each, and with Crosslands missing he seemed to bear the main brunt of the bowling. With his batting now, sadly, taking what seemed to be second place, nothing could stop his complete supremacy over opposing batsmen. The year 1888 was quite remarkable. His tally of 160 wickets included feats like 13 wickets in the match against Middlesex, 12 v Gloucestershire and 13 versus the touring Australians. Poor Derbyshire were dismissed for 17 with Johnny Briggs finishing with match figures of 13–39. These performances probably acted like a soothing balm to his spiritual injuries gathered the year before at Bradford. Yorshire massacred their rivals with 434 for 2 wickets on the first day—J.B. 1 for 194! Wisden for 1888 saw fit to include Briggs in their Six Bowlers of the Year, along with Peel, Woods, Lohmann, Ferris and Turner.

The Roses games provided Johnny Briggs with that extra challenge of ability and moments of nerve tingling excitement, moments of head to head tussles against the best opposition. At Headingly, in 1893, a low scoring game saw Briggs taking eight wickets for 19 runs, while on the August Bank Holiday of the following year, Old Trafford seethed like a cauldron when Briggs prepared to bowl the last ball to big hitting George Ulyett, with Yorkshire wanting six runs to win. Briggs gambled bravely when tossing it high to invite the slog. The bowler was not to be disappointed, for Ulyett slammed the ball high towards the boundary, only for Wood to catch it miraculously near the fence. Neville Cardus explained how Johnny Briggs sat in the pavilion afterwards all white and tense, following his dice with death. It was a toss-up who was the best slow left arm spinner at this time, because Briggs' greatest rival was Bobby Peel of Yorkshire. Many thought Peel more difficult to score from with his immaculate flight and length, but Briggs was always prepared to invite batsmen to commit suicide from his copious variety of deliveries. In pre-First World War cricket, it was quite acceptable to open the bowling with spin and pace, hence Briggs' initial opening partner was the ill fated Crossland. Later Arthur Mold, who was just as fast and questionable, completed the ideal combination.

From 391 appearances Johnny Briggs' wicket tally for Lancashire amounted to well over 1,600, costing only 15.65 each, which put him second in the county records to Brian Statham's 1,800. He is the only Lancashire player to make 11,000 runs, and take 1,000 wickets. Inevitably such statistics include memorable feats of outstanding performances. He took all 10 wickets for 55 runs v Worcester in 1900, at Old Trafford, after narrowly missing the ultimate with 9–29 against Derbyshire at Derby in 1885, and in the game v Sussex, at Old Trafford in 1888, he claimed 9–88. Incidentally, in 1890, Lancashire scored 246–2 against the latter county, with Johnny making 129 not out, but when Sussex batted they couldn't overcome Briggs and Watson, who bowled unchanged throughout the match, and were dismissed for 35 and 24. Their analyses are interesting:

	1st Innings				2nd Innings			
	O	M	R	W	O	M	R	W
Watson	27	21	7	5	19.4	16	6	4
Briggs	27	18	25	5	19	11	16	5

It was Johnny Briggs' good fortune to complete a double hat-trick at Parkfield one day, but to clean bowl all six made the occasion more exceptional. He achieved a single hat-trick in the North v South encounter at Scarborough, in 1891. Such successes are not so surprising when considering he took all 10 wickets three times, 100 victims in a season 12 times, and five years he exceeded 150.

On occasions, Johnny Briggs, like many more bowlers of his era, ran up against the mighty bat of W. G. Grace, but few could claim to have bowled 'The Champion' 10 times. Many ploys, some quite devious, were used to overcome Grace's supremacy, such as the time 'Monkey' Hornby tried to move a fielder unobtrusively while Briggs was about to deliver the ball. The resulting stroke was accompanied by the batsman's squeaky voice, "I know what you're doing, Monkey!" During another Gloucestershire v Lancashire battle on the Ashley Down ground at Bristol, Johnny Briggs' first ball was despatched by the Doctor over the football stand, whereupon the smiling bowler walked down the wicket to shake his hand. The next ball took the same route only to be acknowledged again by a handshake. The third, of similar appearance, was meant to follow the other two, but a rattle of the stumps registered an air shot, and Johnny's outstretched hand was not accepted by the retreating Grace, who was not amused!

It was W. G. Grace who once described Johnny as ". . . a conjuror with a ball."

When assessing such extraordinary talent it may have been surprising for many fans to find Johnny Briggs the unassuming character that he was. He had twin sons whom he doted on, and a brother, Joseph who actually played a few games for Nottinghamshire in 1888, as another left-arm bowler. Johnny's second love was billiards, at which he proved more than capable, and it was probably the combination of the two sports that fostered his enjoyment of a glass of ale. He was not known to over indulge, but Hornby, the Lancashire skipper one day questioned his sobriety. Quite shocked Johnny Briggs proceeded to give a trick cycling display in front of the pavilion to ease his viewing captain's anxiety!

As in all other games the Gents v Players fixtures were enhanced by his presence. After his debut in 1884 at the Oval, Johnny Briggs claimed 56 victims in 16 matches. Apart from making many valuable runs, his bowling was predominantly the Players' master weapon. On five occasions he took five wickets in an innings, and three times four scalps. When Charles Kortright, the Essex pace-man made his first appearance at Lords in 1893, the onlookers, except Johnny, were amused to see one of the latter's stumps sent cartwheeling 18 yards!

As early in his career as 1884 Johnny made his first visit to Australia with the Shaw/Shrewsbury side, and soon made his mark with a marvellous 121 at Melbourne, in the second Test Match. This was his first of six tours down-under; only Colin Cowdray in later years has been so often. When England won by 13 runs in the 1st Test at Sydney during the 1887–88 tour, Briggs had a match top score of just 32 in the second innings. It was a game of low scores, but Johnny's contribution was marked by the presentation of a gold medal set in seven diamonds, from the Prince of Wales. This valuable prize was graciously donated to the safe keeping of the Old Trafford pavilion by Mr. Olwen Isherwood when the North played the South there in 1923. Johnny Briggs, because of ill health, didn't go again until W. G. Grace skippered Lord Sheffield's side there in 1891–2. A hat-trick in Johnny's match figures of 12–136 at Adelaide, in the third Test, ensured England's victory. It was during this trip that he claimed his 50th Test wicket. Two years later at Sydney, the first Test seemed to be going all Australia's way, when only 64 runs were needed on the last day with eight wickets in hand. Heavy overnight rain produced the dreaded 'sticky', but when Peel (6–67) and Briggs (3–25) had finished them off, Australia were still 11 short. This had been an outstanding all round exhibition by Johnny Briggs, which included knocks of 57 and 42.

Johnny Briggs was a member of the first English side to tour South Africa, in 1888–89, under the leadership of C. Aubrey Smith. The home players could find no answer to Johnny's puzzling flight and change of pace. His liking for the matting surfaces are shown in his tour tally of a little under 300 wickets, costing only five runs each. In one game versus a twenty-two he took 15 victims at a cost of four runs, and had final figures of 27 wickets for 23 runs! In the Cape Town Test his 7–17 and 8–11 only needing the umpire's help with one l.b.w., all the rest were bowled!

Of his home Tests the Lords match of 1886 is probably an example of hunches proving the right choice. After England had amassed 434 (Briggs 53) Australia made a solid start to their reply. Slightly desperate England captain, A. G. Steel, experimented with Johnny, who demolished the Aussies with 5–29. following on they were again routed by his 6–45, and lost by an innings. How strange when one considers the position of him not being able to 'get on' at Manchester in the previous Test. It doesn't alter the fact that Johnny Briggs is the only Englishman to score a century and take a hat-trick of wickets against Australia. It was the fateful third Test Match at Leeds, in 1899, when, after reaching 3–53 off 30 overs (11 maidens) at the close of play, he was struck down by his perpetual threat of brain malfunction—an epileptic spasm.

It was understood that he suffered a slight fit on the field of play, but a much more severe attack happened in the light-hearted atmosphere of the Empire Music Hall, at Leeds, that same evening. Many observations as to the cause of these breakdowns were debated including the pressure building as he approached his 100th Test victim (he had claimed 97), and a few weeks before he had been injured from a blow over the heart from a hard hit drive off Surrey's Tom Hayward. He attended Cheadle Asylum for eight months, after which he appeared to make a remarkable recovery. Indeed, during the next year of 1900, he performed to his previous high standards, and turned in several notable feats—remember him taking all 10 Worcestershire wickets? Sadly, this short respite ended with yet another attack, and he returned to the asylum, only to die ten months later, aged just 39. It was said he bowled over after over along the ward, and smilingly told the nurses in the evening of another amazing analysis; how comforting to think he enjoyed his cricket to the last, even when so mentally disturbed.

Archie MacLaren, England's captain in the third Test Match at Adelaide, 1902, received the sad news of his old county colleague's demise. Lancashire cricket was never quite the same for a considerable time after, because such natural entertainers blossom but rarely.

Johnny Briggs' funeral service was read by H. R. Napier, another Lancashire cricketer, while many notable cricketing colleagues filled the church to pay their last respects in silent thanksgiving. Johnny would have loved the numerous floral tributes, but the one he would probably have cherished most was in the team's colours of his last tour to Australia. The accompanying message was signed by the revered skipper of that side—A. E. Stoddart.

CHAPTER NINE

Tom Emmett
(England & Yorkshire C.C.C.) 1841–1904

TOM Emmett was born at Crib Lane, Halifax on September 3, 1841 and as a lad his cricket skills gradually matured during countless hours of practice with his young friends. Their wickets were pitched in front of the concrete pillars which formed the entrance to the carriage drive of a wealthy local manufacturer, and a constant watch had to be kept for the sudden appearance of the owner or the local policeman. Tom's first club was Illingworth but it was not long before he joined the Halifax Club as a professional and was paid 2s. 6d. a match. In 1863 Keighley required his services and around 1866 he played for the local twenty two's against the mighty touring All England Elevens.

The first milestone of an illustrious career was reached when he was asked to play for Yorkshire against Surrey at The Oval in 1866. He arrived wearing clogs and carrying his first cricket bag which consisted of the current edition of the Halifax Courier; by this time he was 25 years old. The following year, 1867, saw Tom turn in his first real bowling performance of note, namely 6—7 off 12 balls in the second innings of the County game with Surrey at Bramall Lane, Sheffield.

Bowling fast left arm with a round arm action, Tom moved the ball from the leg to the off and was notorious for the number of wides he bowled. Once Lord Hawke enquired if he was aware of how many wides he had delivered that season, and upon being told 45, Tom replied "Good, give me the ball, my Lord, and I'll soon earn talent money!"—he went on to total 55 wides that year. W. G. Grace, with a wry smile, wondered if it was planned tactics to bowl so many wides and, suddenly, put in a good straight one. It was Grace's opinion that many umpires let his wides go uncalled but, in Tom's opinion they were exaggerated, for he doubted if he ever sent one down much wider than point! Most of his wides came at the beginning of his bowling spells, so much so that they were known as "Tom's preliminary canter".

55

Tom Emmett

He had a marvellous knack of being able to bowl the ball pitching on the leg stump and moving away to hit the top of the off one—he called it his 'sostenutor'. When asked why, he snapped "What else could you call it?" He dismissed W.G. with this ball on a number of occasions, causing the great man to have a high regard for his ability. Weighing 11½ stones and standing 5′ 8″ in height Tom was a chunky character with endless stamina, for in many matches he bowled unchanged either with George Ulyett or George Freeman as his partner. Richard Daft summed him up admirably, saying "he was all wire and whipcord, one of the very best bits of stuff a cricketer was ever made of". Stories, together with wicket-taking feats were legion, for he was the life and soul of any gathering and was well liked by both the professionals and amateurs of his day. Recognised as a complete cricketer, Tom was an agile fielder in the slips or gully, and a powerful driver who scored many useful runs. Alas he tended to be quite reckless at the beginning of his innings, for he would play the ball and run regardless of its proximity. He was noted for taking short singles but never to that eminent cover point the Rev. Vernon Royle. Once when his partner wanted to run he pointed towards the reverend gentleman and roared in a rich Yorkshire brogue "Noa—it's gone to t'plaace". Some versions have it as 'policeman'.

Old pictures depict Tom standing holding the ball and smartly dressed with a neat spotted tie under a butterfly collar. His ruddy face sported a well trimmed moustache and was topped by his cap which was perched dead centre. His rather prominent nose was reponsible for the fairer sex referring to him as 'Punch'. Appearances can be deceptive, for Tom, on a few occasions, had cause to lose his head momentarily. In one particular game he missed a caught and bowled offered by W. G. Grace himself. Tom took off his cap and stamped on it, then proceeded to kick the ball well past the boundary. Regretting his actions he spent the rest of the day apologising to the Doctor. During a club match early in his career a spate of catches were grounded and he threw the ball down shouting "I'm not bowling any more. There's an epidemic on this ground, but thank God, it ain't catching".

In 1878 Tom was elected skipper of Yorkshire and proved a most likeable and competent officer of the Club. Unfortunately he had a tendency not to bowl himself enough which was verified by the Surrey match of 1881 at The Oval. He had used other bowlers to break up a niggling partnership without success and finally taking the ball himself he proceeded to virtually win the game for Yorkshire by taking 8 wickets for 22 runs. At the end of the match many of the watching Yorkshire enthusiasts grabbed Tom and tried to carry him off shoulder high, but he urged them to put him down as they would spill the 'brass' from his bulging pockets. Complying with his request, he was able to reach the safety of the pavilion—the ruse worked for his pockets were never full. Tom rated this as his best ever performance with the ball.

Such was the high ability of the Emmett/Freeman partnership that W. G. Grace considered that 50 made against this pair was always well earned. The Lords wicket of 1870 was notoriously rough—the year of the Summers fatality—and when M.C.C. played Yorkshire these two bowlers gave the Doctor a torrid time, hitting him many times about the body. George Freeman and Tom marvelled at Grace's wonderful innings of 66 under such conditions. Tom seemed to be plagued by the ever present Doctor, as were very many others of this era. As Tom's first encounter with W.G. approached he commented "It's all very well Grace scoring all these runs against the South Country bowling—just wait 'til he comes to Sheffield and samples Freeman and myself". Grace came and scored 122, only for Tom to suggest he should be made to play with a 'littler bat'. The Gloucestershire v Yorkshire game at Cheltenham in 1876 saw W.G. score 318 only to be followed by the inevitable 'Emmettism'—"Grace before meat, Grace after meat, and Grace all bloody day!" A more pleasant meeting took place, again the venue was Lords, when Tom met the Doctor in the road approaching the ground before play began. W.G. informed Tom that in his bag he carried his recently acquired Finals Diploma. During the game Tom had the misfortune to stumble on the wet turf in trying to stop a cover drive from the 'old man'. Upon W.G. enquiring if he was unhurt, Tom pointed to his mud covered seat stating "It's alright Doctor, I've just got *my* Diploma".

Tom disliked close fielders when he was batting and in a game with Kent at Canterbury he pointed out to Lord Harris, who was standing close in on the leg side, that he should move if he valued his life as he had killed many men in that position. This particular game was played on a sticky wicket and tiny Alec Hearne had been striking Tom about the body quite frequently, only for him to walk up the wicket and stop the bowler in his run up. "Wait a minute, my little man, let's straighten the carpet a little". Another daring fieldsman was ordered to "Stand back a bit, mister, for when I hits there I hits adjectival hard".

His popularity and respect was not only reflected by the attitudes of the players, but reached as far as the critical Yorkshire crowds. One murky day at Bramall Lane they actually started to jeer Tom for refusing to take a quick single. Completely unruffled, he addressed them from the middle upon the virtues of letting him mind his own business—the game recommenced amid a background of apologetic noises from the paying customers. At this period Yorkshire had a good wicket-keeper in the popular David Hunter, but for a Scarborough game the selectors picked G. A. R. Leitham instead. He was also a capable player, but the crowd barracked him each time he touched the ball. Tom stopped the game, walked casually across to the noisiest part of the ground, and in a friendly tone, said "Nah, lads, Scarborough has allus had a reputation for being respectable. Don't lose your character". There was no more trouble that day.

Tom Emmett skippered Yorkshire for five years from 1878 to 1882 and in 1883 and 1884 he shared the post with Lord Hawke. Tom proved to be the last professional captain of the county until J. V. Wilson in 1960. During 23 seasons as a Yorkshire cricketer, he scored merely 6,686 runs with an average of 15.4 but took 1,271 wickets averaging 12.68 runs each. In all first class games Tom took 1,500 wickets at well under 14 runs per victim.

His best years were:
1867 – 40 wickets. Average 5.36
1868 – 59 wickets. Average 8.57
1874 – 99 wickets. Average 11.82
1877 – 72 wickets. Average 13.68
1878 – 112 wickets. Average 11.46
1879 – 54 wickets. Average 10.26
1882 – 95 wickets. Average 10.94
1884 – 107 wickets. Average 11.73
1886 – 132 wickets. Average 12.91

His excellent performance in 1886 was achieved at the age of 45.

The year 1869 saw Tom setting a Yorkshire record when he scattered 16 Cambridgeshire batsmen for 38 runs. A benefit was arranged in 1887 from which the admirable sum of £620 was handed to him. Surely, no county club has ever had a more devoted servant.

The combination of Tom Emmett's humour, personality and ability made him a 'must' for touring captains to have in their ranks. The first invitation came from John Lillywhite to visit Australia in 1876, followed by Lord Harris' call in 1878 to return to the Antipodes. Travel in the early ships was sometimes quite hazardous, and poor Tom proved to be a bad sailor spending most of the voyage prostrate. Towards the end of the second Australian journey he ventured on to the deck, where he was confronted by Lord Harris. Glancing at the calm sea Tom passed the comment that he doubted if they had had the heavy roller on yet.

This touring party of 1878 included George Ulyett and Tom as the only professionals, and the latter had a great tour, taking 137 wickets for an average of 8.68 runs and easily topping the bowling table. When the visitors played New South Wales at Sydney an ugly incident occured. After a New South Welshman was adjudged run out, the spectators invaded the pitch seeking some form of retribution. Lord Harris was struck with a stick, but the culprit was immediately 'collared' by 'Monkey' Hornby, and taken to the pavilion. Tom and George Ulyett grabbed a stump each and cleared a path for his Lordship to leave the field safely.

In 1879 Tom crossed the Atlantic to Canada and the U.S.A. under the capable leadership of Richard Daft, and in 1882 he returned to Australia with Alfred Shaw's team.

Having reached the twilight of his career Tom sought quieter pastures and accepted an engagement at Bradford. Then followed his appointment as cricket coach in 1889 at Rugby School on the recommendation of Lord Harris. Sir Pelham Warner, then a pupil at the school, attributed all his cricket 'know-how'—and this was abundant—to Tom Emmett's tutoring. Many times Sir Pelham saw Tom grab a stump at the fall of a wicket and proceed to demonstrate to all interested the final error of the retreating batsman. This cricketing enthusiast was well liked by all the pupils at Rugby, and the staff held him in great esteem. Moving on to Leicester C.C.C. in 1896, he took up his last appointment.

On June 29, 1904, Tom Emmett passed quietly away, and so the triumphs of this Yorkshire idol came to a close. Whenever cricket is discussed, his name, and the stories connected with him, will often be heard.

CHAPTER TEN

W. W. Read
(England & Surrey) 1855–1907

THE appointment of Charles W. Alcock as full time secretary to the Surrey Cricket Club in 1872 was the impetus the team needed. In 1869 only three games were won, while in 1871 only one victory was registered, so spirits were obviously at a low ebb at the Oval when the new secretary took up his position—a post he held with distinction for the next thirty years. Surrey recorded just five losses from fifteen games that year which was highlighted by a five wicket victory over the M.C.C. at Lords. At one stage the M.C.C.'s first innings of 16 showed the scoreboard 0–7–0; surely one of their best wins ever. The second omen of good fortune for Surrey arrived in the form of a well built seventeen year old, who made his debut in 1873. Against the tough opposition of Yorkshire, the youngster batted to make three and fourteen, but in the next game with Kent, he batted at number three to score an impressive 39. Haygarth, in his M.C.C. Scores and Biographies for 1873, included this forecast in his biographical note on the new arrival ". . . bidding fair, if he continues the game, to arrive at the top of the tree". Such profound words were to be wholly fulfilled some years later, for the lad's name was Walter Read.

Born at Reigate, in 1855, Walter Read followed in his father's footsteps as a schoolteacher, and was to assist the latter at Reigate School. Typically Victorian, the headmaster was a strict disciplinarian with regard to his son, which restricted Walter to play only in the summer holidays, for Surrey. For the next eight years these spasmodic appearances only whetted the Surrey supporters appetites to want to see more of this attractive strokemaker. Such an occasion was an opening partnership with Read and Jupp of 206 against Yorkshire at the Oval, in 1877. Having shot out the opposition for 159, Surrey were frustrated by rain, with the abandonment coming after Jupp had finally made 87 and Read 140. This same year Walter Read made his first appearance for the Gents at Princes ground. Although overshadowed by W. G. Grace's 134, Read's 72 impressed everyone, espec-

W. W. Read

ially against the top class bowling of Hill, Emmett, Ulyett, Southerton and Mycroft. The young aspirant must have gleaned tremendous
pleasure and know-how, from such a long partnership with the celebrated doctor, but it was to be five years before Walter was able to
play for the Gents again.

When Walter Read was made assistant secretary to C. W. Alcock
in 1881, Surrey cricket acquired the regular services of its new admi-
nistrator, for he hardly missed a game in the next 16 years. The
cockney supporters had now to distinguish Walter Read from Maurice Read, the Surrey professional, so they nicknamed the former
'Walla Walla', soon to be abbreviated to 'W.W.' Their new idol was
just short of six feet tall, and rising to 14 stones in weight, but he was
a broad shouldered man with a cheerful, reserved nature. At times he
could be quite argumentative, but his fighting spirit on the field never
wavered from the line of fairness. Surrey's followers loved to see him
settle into his upright stance, the launching pad for his thunderous
strokes off the back foot, tremendous square cuts and drives between
cover and point, but, possibily his most notorious shot,—the pull.
Batsmen, such as Ranji, Trumper and Hirst, were to use this shot in
later years, but 'W.W.' was the recognised pioneer. In its early days
the stroke was quite 'agricultural', with a good eye essential, and
must have seemed a little out of place in 'W.W.'s normally straight-
batted technique. C. B. Fry, in his book 'Life Worth Living', tells
how Ranji related to him that Walter Read actually showed the
Prince how to play the pull shot in the nets, but 'C.B.' hastily added
that Ranji had too many other safer shots, to indulge regularly in such
risks. In his book 'Recollections and Reminiscences' Lord Hawke recalls
that 'W.W.' never turned down the chance to gamble with the stroke. It
was at Bramall Lane that Lord Hawke dropped the Surrey 'crack', as
he was known, after atempting to pull Tom Emmett. The Yorkshire
crowd gave the fielder some terrible 'stick', but Emmett simply asked
the downcast Lord Hawke to move "a little more west, Sir". The very
next ball was pulled powerfully to the same place where the distraught
Lord Hawke brought off a superb one handed catch, and could do no
wrong at Sheffield for a considerable time afterwards!

Follwing his rapid improvement from playing regularly, it was no
surprise when 'W.W.' was selected to tour Australia with the Hon.
Ivor Bligh's team of 1882–3. This very strong side was to recover
'The Ashes', and put English cricket back on top. In the second Test,
at Melbourne, Bates bowled his slow-medium off-cutters superbly for
match figures of 14 for 102. His 7 for 28 in the first innings included a
hattrick with the wickets of McDonnell, Giffen and Bonnor. At the
dismissal of the second victim, it was decided in the mid-wicket

discussion, that Bonnor would play defensively at his first ball.
Bonnor, it must be remembered, was one of the games's hardest
hitters, but Walter Read was the brave fielder to creep in slowly from
short mid-on. The Australian batsman, as a rabbit hypnotised by a
stoat, gently played the ball in to 'W.W.'s waiting hands! England
won by 27 runs. When the visitors travelled to play eighteen of
Maryborough in Queensland, they were one of the first touring sides
to visit the northern state. Local enthusiasm was unbounded, so much
so that the authorities put up a plot of land as a prize for the tourist
making the highest individual score—Walter Read became a Queensland freeholder with 66!

Back home 'W.W.' was responsible for Surrey's revival, such a
revival was to be a build-up to the County Championship, a little
later. His value to the side, apart from his batting expertise, could be
found in his consistent fielding at point, occasional lob-bowling to
break a partnership even in a test match, and a wicket-keeping ability
of high quality to fill an emergency. In 'W.W.'s first full season,
1881, he 'kept' against Yorkshire, at Huddersfield, and didn't let a
bye through in a total of 388, while at the 1891 Scarborough Festival,
for the Gentlemen of England versus Sherwin's Notts XI, he did the
hattrick with his lobs. Walter Read really set out his stall in 1881 with
delights like his 160 against Kent, at Maidstone, which included three
sixes and 29 fours. Surrey became the first team to notch up a total
of over 500 against a team of touring Australians. This feat was in
1886, and with 'W.W.' contributing a notable 80, after Maurice
Read's 186 and Bobby Abel's 144, Surrey's 501 was enough to
achieve an innings and 209 runs victory.

The year 1887 was to be a memorable one. Walter Read, now
skipper, brought the Championship back to the Oval after 14 years,
and it was to stay there for nine of the following 12 years. John
Shuter had been a popular skipper before this, and with W. W.
Read, Bobby Abel and George Lohmann, was the cornerstone of
Surrey's surge to the title. This same year 'W.W.' made 247 and 244
not out in successive games against Cambridge University and Lancashire. Inevitably, Surrey's top batsman found himself on the boat to
Australia again, at the end of the season, under the leadership of
Lord Hawke. The party was managed by G. F. Vernon, and W. W.
Read dominated the batting with three centuries from his 610 runs
from eight games: he topped the averages with 55.45. Unfortunately,
another team, led by Lillywhite, Shaw and Shrewsbury, toured at the
same time, and when asked to reconsider, before embarking, the
three pro's refused. Financial disaster befell both sides. At the end of
the tour both teams combined under the leadership of Walter Read,

to beat Australia, at Sydney by 126 runs. 'W.W.' returned to England in 1888, and that summer again was outstanding for him. If Oxford University were having a quiet smirk about Cambridge's onslaught from Walter Read's bat the previous season, they were in for a rude awakening. From a Surrey total of 650 at the Oval, he amassed his highest score of 338, containing 46 fours. When the Gentlemen of England met the Australians at Lords, W. G. Grace's 165 and Read's 109 in a score of 490 must have been well worth seeing. Turner and Ferris had been bowling out most of the county sides, but this partnership proved overwhelming.

In the winter of 1891–2, Walter Read captained a side to South Africa, and proved far too strong for the opposition. The only Test match was won by an innings and 189 runs, with Ferris (the Australian was now playing for Gloucestershire) taking 13 for 91, and Surrey's keeper, H. Wood, making 134, his only first class hundred. 'W.W.' proved a most popular skipper, and was respected by all his fellow players. Of his home Tests Walter Read made useful scores, but nothing to catch the eye—except in 1884, at the Oval. Although feeling unwell, 'W.W.' was cross with Lord Harris for putting him in at number ten, and the Australians weren't too pleased when he proceeded to smash 117 in just over two hours; the score was 8 for 181 when he went in. In an innings noted for its superb leg-side hittings, Spofforth missed a half chance of caught and bowled when Walter Read was 23, and many thought it the best display of on-side play since the days of George Parr. During the Tests of 1888 the Athletic News asked its readers to select 'A Model England Team', and W. G. Grace and W. W. Read were the only unanimous choices.

After the five year gap between his first and second games for the Gents, 'W.W.' played regularly another 22 times until 1896. He made over 1,100 runs, which included eight half centuries, and reaching the 40's on three other occasions. It was Walter Read's turn, in 1884, to be part of a hattrick performed by Richard Barlow, at the Oval— W. G. Grace and John Shuter were the other two. Immediatley afterwards, at Lords, 'W.W.' put on 163 for the fifth wicket with Lord Harris, in less than two and a half hours (Harris 85, Read 67). The following year saw Walter Read make his highest score in the Gents v Players fixture. An absorbing partnership with Grace of 135 for the third wicket, in the second innings, eventually ended to the onlookers disappointment, but 'W.W.' went on to make 159. Walter Read captained the Gents in 1892, at the Oval, and celebrated with a brilliantly made 70 out of 182, a feat more meritorious when considering he was up against the bowling might of Lockwood, Lohmann and Peel. In the same game, while fielding in his usual position at point, Bobby Abel cut hard to wind him badly, the game being held up for three minutes. This friendly rivalry between the two Surrey idols continued in the September game, at Scarborough, the same year. After Abel had miraculously caught Read at short slip in the Gents' first innings, Read proceeded to dismiss Abel, caught and bowled off his lobs for five, much to Abel's embarrassment! The thrilling one wicket victory of the Gents at the Oval, in 1896, was set up with Walter Read's solid 56 in their first innings. This proved to be 'W.W.' last Gents game—a fitting swan-song for one of the fixture's favourite players. Walter Read was one of Surrey's greatest cricketers, and although he played for England at Test level, for the Gentlemen in that prestigious of fixtures, his forte was county cricket. Three times, in 1883, 1886 and 1888, he headed the national batting averages. Surrey brought home the title in 1892 for the third year running, with 13 wins from 16 matches, and 'W.W.' contributed all of Surrey's three centuries that season. Surrey's Jubilee year was 1895, and after 29 years the Surrey v England fixture was revived. As a mark of respect to their outstanding star the committee allowed Walter Read to make this his benefit game. The season of 1897 was W.W. Read's, and George Lohmann's last with the county, and the former's final game was against the old foe, Yorkshire, 'W.W.' made 46 centuries in important games, 37 for Surrey, together with one treble and three double centuries. He scored over 1,000 runs a season on nine occasions, and well above 22,000 in first class games.

Apart from his cricketing prowess, Walter Read's sporting capabilities reflected many other facets. His accomplished feats as a skater and walker vied with those moments of outstanding skill on the football field or the billiard table. Many a winter's afternoon he tramped copse and stubble to practice his expertise with a gun, and often in the company of Ranji and C. B. Fry. Such friendships were commonplace with 'W.W.' and his death in 1907, at Addiscombe, at the very early age of 51 years, devastated his many acquaintances and admirers. The late nineteenth century Surrey equivalent to Peter May had passed away, but supporters' adulation for him continued, and could be aptly remembered from a cockney verse by 'The Man On The Spot', for an edition of the Sporting Life, at the time of Walter Read's heyday.

"See him make his boundary hits,
He ain't the sort to play for nuts:
Hook 'em here and carves 'em there,
Bangs 'em off and hits 'em square;
And when I shed my little bob,
I like to see him on the job".

CHAPTER ELEVEN

A. G. Steel
(England & Lancashire) 1858–1914

It was A. G. Steel's father's ambition that his fifth son of seven should join brother D.Q. at Uppingham School, but when his letter to the housemaster requesting this position was left unanswered, Marlborough College reaped rich rewards from the cricketing prowess of its new pupil. Steel quickly developed into one of the greatest schoolboy cricketers ever, indeed he was almost good enough to play for the Gents in his last year. This unique youngster played for the College from 1874 to 1877, and when skipper of the side in '76 and '77, Marlborough only lost one game. Making many runs and taking consistently high tallies of wickets with quickish leg-spin, W. G. Grace thought him the best schoolboy cricketer he had ever seen. A. G. Steel bowled much quicker then, almost medium paced, and used a very fast ball as an effective surprise. It was considered that his bowling in 1877 and 1878 was never bettered in the following years of great success.

'Nab', as he was later nicknamed, was a true Lancastrian. Born at Liverpool in the September of 1858, he became one of the county's brightest lights, but before such heady occasions he went up to Trinity Hall, Cambridge, in 1878, and dominated the University's batting and bowling averages for the next four seasons. No Freshman before had achieved such notoriety. W. G. Grace went to Cambridge University to watch Steel play in a game when the latter made almost a century, and the 'Grand 'Ol' Man's' assessment of the youngster's ability was how just half an hour in the nets with him was all that was needed.

It is thought that the Cambridge side of 1878 was probably the strongest Varsity side ever, because their record of eight matches, including one against the touring Australians, were all won. In a special match that season, to open Liverpool's new ground at Aigburgh, the University visitors beat Lancashire convincingly with A. G. Steel taking 6–22 and 5–91, to give his county a fore-taste of its future acquisition. With stars like the Hon. Alfred and the Hon.

A. G. Steel

Edward Lyttleton, A. P. Lucas and A. G. Steel batting number seven, Cambridge University had little difficulty in defeating Oxford University by 238 runs. 'Nab's' contributions consisted of a first innings knock of 44, with bowling figures of 8–62 and 5–11. There were some superb all-round seasons to follow, but 1878, when he topped the first class bowling averages with 164 wickets, costing just 9 runs each, was an achievement of the topmost class for any nineteen year old. A. G. Steel ended with 75 wickets for Cambridge University at only 7 runs each, while a very respectable batting average of 37 fully justified his billing as a future allround star. The following year he was fourth in the national batting averages among a host of highly skilled batsmen.

Oxford again felt the full brunt of Steel's ability in 1879 with a nine wickets defeat after 'Nab' had scored 64 and match bowling figures of 11–66, including the hat trick. In the pre-Varsity match games, the next season, A. G. Steel made a memorable 118 against Surrey at the Oval. This was an admirable warm-up and an Oxford warning, for he had Varsity match figures of ten wickets for 98 runs each in a masterly Cambridge win. This victory was sweet indeed, for 'Nab' was that year's Cambridge skipper. Oxford, in Steel's last year, 1881, gained a welcome 135 run win, but not before Steel had played his heart out in an attempt to deny them victory with a four wicket tally in the first innings for 46 runs, and a Cambridge top score of 36 in the second innings.

Deceptively turning the ball both ways, but mainly from the leg, A. G. Steel took 38 wickets in his four Varsity matches, and scored 184 runs. The Hon. Alfred Lyttleton, a life-long friend, kept wicket to Steel and found his deliveries very difficult to decipher. 'Nab' Steel possessed an ice-cool temperament, but his amiable nature made him a favourite among fellow players all of his short career. On an occasion when Cambridge University met Yorkshire, Steel teased Tom Emmett in a friendly manner when asking the wily old Tyke bowler to send him down a "good one", and a half crown would be the prize if the delivery bowled him. Steel struggled hard to keep it out from his wicket, which caused Tom Emmett to laugh and call out, "she was worth 15 (old) pence when she were on the way, Sir!" Although winning captains are usually popular, some of their small mis-calculations are often overlooked. This was forcibly brought home to Steel when Surrey played Lancashire at Manchester in 1887. W. E. Roller and Walter Read put on 305 in four hours for Surrey, which brought the inquisitive Steel to ask the former why he had never player for Cambridge University. Steel's shame was complete when the Surrey run-maker replied, "Because you never asked me!"

Steel represented his University in the doubles at rackets; his partner was the Hon. Ivor Bligh, in 1880.

A. G. Steel, while still at Marlborough in 1877, had made his distinguished debut for Lancashire, with a fine 87 against Sussex. Such was his youthful expertise that he was considered almost good enough to play for England. Using a slightly crouched right-hand stance, he was prepared to attack all bowlers in a style of his own. Watching the ball very closely, his footwork brought him to its pitch quickly, from where he seldom lofted his shots, preferring to pierce the field with strokes along the ground. Perhaps his only slight weakness was in catching, and this, it was understood, was because of a mild short-sightedness, a malady that the Hon. Alfred Lyttleton attributed to the reason why he used a crouched stance to peer at the approaching ball more closely. Luckily for the bowlers he only just managed to 'struggle' along with impaired vision! Although never able to play regularly for Lancashire, indeed he never played a full season, Steel was able to pick up his bat after any interval of time from the game, and play a majestic innings. Such miracles of technique and timing were bestowed upon later stars such as F. S. Jackson, A. C. MacLaren, and later still, the Rt. Rev. David Shepherd and Cyril Washbrook.

A brilliant legal brain took A. G. Steel to the Bar in 1883, and as a K.C. he concentrated his practice on Admiralty cases in the Liverpool courts. However, he was able to fit many county games into his busy life, and Yorkshire was to suffer most from his ability to make runs and take wickets, after lengthy periods of inactivity. With a total lack of nervousness, A. G. Steel thrived on batting and bowling against top opposition, and it seemed he saved his best for the 'Old Enemy', Yorkshire. He didn't play in a great number of Roses games, but what an impract he was to make upon the fixture.

In Steel's great year of 1878, he had match bowling figures of 14–112 in the Old Trafford game, and this included his finest tally of 9–63 in the second innings. Again on his home ground, in 1879, Steel took 7–34 enabling Lancashire to gain an innings victory. At Sheffield, the following season he took 7–43, while at Old Trafford in 1881, he matched 13 wickets with a superb 50 not out from 178 to win the game by eight wickets. Approaching the entrance gate turnstiles at one Roses game, the genial Tom Emmett enquired of the gateman if A. G. Steel was playing. Receiving a reply in the affirmative, Tom laughingly told his colleagues, "May as well go home, lads, Mr. Steel's playing and Yorkshire's beat!" Such a remark could well have been appropriate in 1886 when Steel scored 55 out of a meagre Lancashire first innings of 112, while in their second knock he slammed a match-winning 80 not out from 178 needed for victory. Tom Emmett and 'Nab' Steel seemed to have a wonderful rapport, with good humoured remarks frequently exchanged. When Lancashire were taking the field on one occasion in 1880, Tom commented on Steel's flapping bootlaces, but, quite unperturbed, 'Nab' pointed out that he wouldn't need any laces in his boots to bowl out Yorkshire— he didn't, when yet again he took seven wickets! Sadly, in such a short career, flashes of his batting brilliance were to be savoured, like his 105 against Surrey at Old Trafford in 1887. For Lancashire he made nearly 2,000 runs, and took over 230 wickets.

Some of his best innings were played for other teams. Often he turned out from the M.C.C. and Ground, and played majestic knocks, like his 106 in 80 minutes on a turning wicket at Scarborough in 1881. The M.C.C. only totalled 181, but it was enough to win by an innings. Lord Hawke commented that it was the finest innings he had seen played. Another noteable knock for the M.C.C. and Ground was his 134 versus the touring Australians at Lords, in 1884. Another side to benefit from this master of stroke play was the Gentlemen of England. Going back, in 1882, to play his old University, he hammered 171, while his bowling in 1878 devastated the Australians when he collected 4–37 and 7–35, and thus made the Gents modest score of 139 enough to win by an innings and one run.

As great as his batting skills were, his bowling held centre stage in his cricketing career of just ten years from 1878 to 1888. It is stated how he bowled his slightly round arm deliveries with eyes wide and expectant, while his nostrils flared with utter determination! Leg-spin at this time was somewhat novel, but his cleverly highflighted bowling caused leading batsmen to check their driving at seemingly innocuous half vollies. To a new batsman it was nothing for him to bowl one wide of the leg stump hoping for a catch deep on the on-side. 'Nab' Steel was always thinking of new ploys to draw batsmen into his intricate web of deception.

Even the most successful bowlers have days when little goes right, and A. G. Steel was no exception. George Bonnor, the Australian giant who made many bowlers suffer from his prodigious blows, caused 'Nab' a few headaches, while W. G. Grace once hit him out of the Scarborough ground, over square leg. Surely his most humiliating moment came at the hands of C. I. 'Buns' Thornton, when the latter played for the Gentlemen of England versus I. Zingari at Scarborough, in 1886. From a Gents total of 266 Thornton made 107 not out after going in with the score at 133 for 5. In 70 minutes, and only 29 scoring strokes, he hit seven sixes out of the ground, including one into Trafalgar Square. Even when facing such relentless aggression, Steel still maintained his masterly flight, hoping against hope for a short cessation of hostilities. Such are the dangers of bowlers when relying on flight and spin, but such a respected authority on cricket as H. S. Altham wrote in 1926 that in his opinion A. G. Steel had been the top leg-spinner up to that point in time.

'Nab' Steel was 22 years of age when he tasted Test cricket, but this was simply due to the fact that the first Test match in this counry wasn't played until 1880. In order to play at the Oval on such an auspicious occasion, Steel interrupted a shooting holiday in Scotland. England's batsmen, when set just 50 runs to win, made a real 'hash' of the start when finding themselves 5–20. Steel, batting at number seven, had changed, but with wickets tumbling he rapidly changed back to his whites—but was not needed. This five wicket win for England was the only Test Match that year, as was the Oval game in 1882. With a narrow seven run victory for Australia came the birth of 'The Ashes' to commemorate the demise of English cricket. Although A. G. Steel was a participant, perhaps his disappointment was appeased with an invitation at the end of the season to tour Australia with the Hon. Ivor Bligh's team. Even when taking 152 scalps on the trip, the firmness of the wickets down under was given as one reason for 'Nab's flight and spin proving moderately unsucessful in Tests. The novel experience of travelling in such a vast Continent, together with the organised social friendliness, made the tour a memorable one; not to mention an overall England victory of two Tests to one.

A. G. Steel saved his best Test knock for the unique setting of Lords, in 1884. He totally shattered the strong Aussie attack of Spofforth, Giffen, Palmer, Midwinter and Boyle in the second Test, with a dashing style seldom seen before or since. Sparkling footwork enabled him to reach Spofforth's slower ball and drive powerfully; much to W. G. Grace's impish enjoyment in seeing 'The Demon' so treated. Having played very little cricket up to that point of the season, this innings of 148 in 2 hours 50 minutes was a masterpiece long since talked of. For sheer cheeky, spirited attack it has ever been a prime example.

When speaking of the earliest Australians to tour here it must be remembered that a large proportion of Englishmen thought them to be black, especially after a team of Aboriginals had toured here earlier, in 1868. This misconception was made apparent to 'Nab' Steel when sitting with Spofforth in the Lords pavilion one day watching the cricket. The Rev. Arthur Wood approached Steel and commented how pleased he was to see that 'Nab' would be playing against the 'niggers' on Monday. Much to Spofforth's amusement 'Nab' introduced him to the non-plussed cleric as "the demon nigger bowler!"

'Nab' Steel had proved a winning captain with Marlborough, Cambridge University, the Gentlemen and England, for in 1886 he took over the skipper's role for his country and was victorious in all three home Tests versus Australia.

For all round ability on the field, both in playing power and tactics, his prowess has seldom been bettered. In later years a batsman like Reggie Spooner and all-rounders F. S. Jackson and Wilfred Rhodes, were frequently compared with A. G. Steel. In all first-class cricket Steel made nearly 7,000 runs, with seven centuries and 788 wickets.

In 18 appearances for the Gentlemen versus the Players at Lords and the Oval, 'Nab' captured 99 wickets at 15 runs each. Strangely, he wasn't very successful with the bat, but there was one game in 1882, at Lords, when he scored 76 and took seven wickets in the match. His six wickets for 60 runs in the Players first innings at the Oval, in 1878, was instrumental in a Gents victory of 55 runs, and he again had 7–27 at the same venue, the following year. This last game is remembered for a notable bowling feat, because he and A. H. Evans bowled unchanged through both players' innings: Evans had 7–31 in the second knock. It must have been a very poignant moment playing his last game for the Gents, which was in 1891 at Lords, for he was made captain. A fitting compliment to one of the fixture's greatest and most popular celebrities.

Cricket to A. G. Steel surely proved a source of great pleasure. He was one of four brothers to play for Lancashire: indeed, there was one special day when all four played at the same match. 'Nab's' son, Alan Ivor, played just two games for Middlesex in 1912, but was sadly killed in action in 1917. Although his practice took him away from the game for considerably long periods, A. G. Steel's interest never waned, even after his last game, which was for the I. Zingari team in 1895. In some ancient team photographs he is shown wearing a flamboyant sash, a tightly buttoned shirt and sporting a pill-box hat in I. Zingari colours. It must have been most awkward to field in. Perhaps it was the difficulty in keeping it on that caused his slight inconsistency when catching, and not his suspected short-sightedness.

In later life Steel's spare time was given to being a member of the M.C.C. Committee, which culminated in the Presidency in 1902. Cricket theories was another field in which he was often quoted, and he was joint author with his life-long friend the Hon. R. H. Lyttleton, of the Badminton book on cricket. 'Nab's' chapter on the wiles of bowling was one of the most enlightening on the subject ever. He was eager to try many changes in the game from narrower bats to wider wickets, not to mention the age-old problem of altering the l.b.w. laws.

The year 1914 will be remembered by all as the commencement of European hostilities, and a time of sadness and great apprehension. It will also be memorable to cricket followers as the year when the game lost R. E. Foster and A. O. Jones, but probably more outstanding was the passing at his Hyde Park home, of A. G. 'Nab' Steel, after the sadly short life-span of just 55 years.

CHAPTER TWELVE

Richard Barlow
(Lancashire C.C.C.) 1850–1919

PROBABLY Richard Barlow's proudest moment on the cricket field was the day in 1875 at Old Trafford, when he and his opening partner, A. N. 'Monkey' Hornby, knocked off the 148 runs Yorkshire had set Lancashire to win. Skipper Hornby made 78 not out and Barlow 50 not out; such a comparable scoring rate by this opening pair was seldom repeated, as Barlow was more notorious for his stubborn methods. He used such a dour style with the sole purpose of bene-fitting his county's performance, because his attitude of "I'm in—you get me out" was one of a dedicated cricketer, performing to his utmost.

Richard Barlow was born at Barrow Bridge, Bolton, on 28 May, 1850. As a youngster he loved ball games, and was soon showing a natural aptitude when swinging a roughly hewn piece of wood at a ball of cloth and string. In old age he remembered these early times as periods of lasting enjoyment; times of youthful abandonment before his more sombre employment in the moulding trade, upon leaving school. These hours of 'piecework' enabled him to rise at 4.30 and complete his tasks early, thus leaving more time to practice his cricket. It was at about this period, after moving to Derbyshire for a brief spell, that Barlow was asked to play for a Staveley and District XXII against George Parr's touring All England XI. After showing more than a little promise, Hickton, of the tourists, advised him to approach Old Trafford for a trial. Before accepting the advice he took the pro's job at Farsley, near Leeds, on the recommendation of Richard Daft—an experience that helped mature his obviously high potential. Such was his rapid progress that Lancashire asked him to join them in 1871—without a trial!

As an ex-club professional, Barlow had worked hard at his bowl-ing, so was now a competent right hand opening batsman, and a respected medium paced, left arm bowler. In his youth he had been a left hand bat, but his father convinced him that all left handers

Richard Barlow

appeared awkward, so he changed to the right. Barlow recalled how very few people watched county cricket at Old Trafford when he first played there, but, with Lancashire's increasing strength and successes, this was soon to change. His first game was against the 'old enemy', Yorkshire, at Sheffield in 1871, and he managed to take a wicket with his first ball. Alec Watson, another fellow county player for many years, was to make his debut that same year. At one stage Barlow's craving to succeed in all the game's departments gave him the urge to try wicket-keeping, but a painful blow from a batsman altered his mind in that direction. Apart from becoming one of the leading all-rounders of that era, his fielding at point was outstanding.

Richard Barlow was a dapper dresser. His King George V styled beard was never trimmed otherwise, and seemed to complement his naturally quiet, contented nature. Total abstinence from drink and cigarettes helped to attain a peak of physical fitness achieved by few, but envied by many. Sadly, his sporting achievements, and popularity, didn't promote a happy marriage, for it was one of unending conflicts, and seldom mentioned. Even to this day a professional cricketer's wife spends a lot of time apart from her husband, and in Barlow's case, the fact that he played football in the winter, didn't help to forge a pleasant relationship. As a goalkeeper, he represented Lancashire, and the North versus the South in a game at Sheffield. In latter years he was a respected referee, and had the dubious honour of refereeing the cup tie between Preston North End and Hyde, at Preston in 1887. He laughingly recalled how, if the Hyde goalkeeper hadn't had a good game, the score could have been worse—Preston 26, Hyde 0!

On numerous occasions Barlow opened the Lancashire innings with Hornby, and with the latter's aptitude for short singles, spectators were entertained to hours of amusement, and betting opportunities on who would run out the other. They were the greatest of run-stealers, but after one instance of indecision Barlow was heard to explain—"first he runs you out of breath, then he runs you out; then he gives you a sovereign"! Such wailings must be considered in the lightest possible way, for the Lancashire captain was the idol of his opening partner. This, surely, was borne out when Barlow dedicated his book of absorbing anecdotes, 'Forty Seasons of First Class Cricket' to his skipper. Years later, when poet Francis Thompson watched the efforts of his Lancashire side at Lords, he finished his verses of heart-felt nostalgia with "Oh my Hornby and my Barlow long ago"!

Richard Barlow was a wonderful judge of length when batting, and using forward defensive strokes, was the original 'stonewaller' of cricket. After Barlow had made 5 runs in 150 minutes at Nottingham in 1882, the Nottinghamshire bowler, William Barnes, couldn't help but show his frustration at the end of the innings, when he gasped, "Bowling at thee were like bowling at a stone wall". Lancashire had been bowled out for 69! Many other bowlers must have experienced the same feeling after striving to dismiss the Lancastrian defender, when playing the 'old man's game', as it was then referred to. In the match against Yorkshire at Bradford, in 1874, he put together 17 in 150 minutes, while in the Sussex game at Old Trafford, in 1876, he 'raced' to 2 runs in 41 minutes in the first innings, and 5 in 150 minutes in the second. Six years later he played his 'stonewall' innings against Notts: perhaps it should be mentioned that he had scored 8 runs in 70 minutes, in the first innings! When Lancashire met Notts at Nottingham, in 1876, the former's first wicket fell at 45 in the first innings, with the scoreboard showing Hornby 45, Barlow not out 0! It seems Notts' bowlers were quite often on the receiving end when Barlow decided to stick, so was it Morley's frustration when appealing for l.b.w. after he had struck Barlow in the middle of his forehead, or was it the umpire's chance to escape the threat of boredom, when he gave him out?

Although Barlow's technique was basically one of defence, there were occasions when he unleashed strokes that surprised even his closest colleagues. His highest score of 117 was made at Lords, in 1884, and included three fours in one over—he batted for three hours. In the same year, playing against Cheshire, at Stockport, Barlow hit a ball out of the ground and into a potato field, from where it was never recovered. Other instances, such as 40 runs out of 95, against Surrey, in 1873, and 56 out of 114 versus Kent, in 1877, just go to prove that he possessed other methods to blunt an attack, apart from dogged defence.

Barlow carried his bat 50 times, and 12 of these were for Lancashire. With Notts again the sufferers, he carried his bat for 44 not out in the first innings of the game at Liverpool, in 1882, then was last out in the second innings when run out for 49; he was on the field when 20 Lancashire wickets fell. After carrying his bat for 29 in three hours at Leicester, in 1889, Barlow attended a dinner afterwards, and gave his rendition of the song "You'll Remember Me". Later, a speaker, on behalf of the hosts, pointed out that they were never likely to forget him! He played in 246 matches for his county, and almost did the double in the Roses games with over 1,000 runs and 86 wickets. Of his seven centuries, five were for Lancashire, and, it was suggested, given the time there would have been more! In 1875 Richard Barlow topped the national batting averages in first class cricket with 38.8 runs per innings. He was the first player to top Lancashire's batting and bowling averages, which he achieved in 1882. In top cricket Barlow made over 8,000 runs, at 14 an hour, while his average of 20 is only slightly less than the more dashing Hornby's. Richard Barlow shared the distinction of never making a 'pair' with W. G. Grace.

It appears that a gentleman named Riley was attracted to Barlow's bowling action, and advised him to concentrate on this other gift. It wasn't long before the youngster was putting down pieces of paper at the pitch of a good length ball, and, mixing slow flight with pace, tried to bowl at the targets. After hours of diligent practice, Barlow started to produce results that over the years made him one of cricket's great all-rounders. The eminent Dr. W. G. Grace was to be his victim 31 times, and on 14 of these occasions the great man was bowled. Bobby Abel, England and Surrey's cockney opener, was another of many who found difficulty in handling Barlow's subtle flight and change of pace. The immaculate length of his bowling, together with away movement to a right-hander, was enough to think about for any in-coming batsman, but probably his most dangerous ball was the 'armer', that drifted disconcertingly. Batsmen were pinned down with uncanny consistency, as the Sussex players were to witness at Manchester, in 1885, when Barlow bowled for an hour for one run.

The statistics of Barlow's bowling performances seem endless, but a few will suffice to illustrate such outstanding talent. In the compilation of just over 800 wickets in first class cricket he did the hat-trick twice. The first was against Derbyshire, at Derby in 1881, while the second, and even more notable event, was for the Players against the Gentlemen at the Oval, in 1884. His three victims were W. G. Grace, J. Shuter and W. W. Read—prime scalps indeed. A best bowling performance of nine for 39 against Sussex, at Manchester, in 1886, must have been under pressure when he took eight wickets for less than 30 runs on another three occasions. His fitness was also tested when bowling unchanged through two consecutive innings twice. His penetrative powers are well illustrated when claiming five wickets for three runs against Kent in 1878, and six for three versus Derbyshire, in 1881.

Richard Barlow's finest allround performance was undoubtedly when the North of England met the touring Australians at Trent Bridge, in 1884. After making 10 not out, he had four wickets for six runs in 24 balls. Spofforth, eyeing a damaged wicket, estimated that the Englishmen wouldn't reach 60 in their second innings, but Barlow proceeded to bat for four and a half hours, making 101 out of a total of 255! They had been five for 53 until Flowers and Barlow put on 158 for the sixth wicket. It would appear that Barlow exploited the wicket's hidden dangers better than the 'Demon', for he took six for 42 in the Australian second innings. Outstanding performances by players during this period were recognised in the form of mementoes and gifts of money from the public, so Barlow duly went home with a diamond tiepin, a claret jug, £10 in cash and the match scorecard printed on satin.

No Players XI, between 1876 and 1886, was complete which didn't include R. G. Barlow. He was to prove a thorn in the side of many Gents teams, because throughout 19 appearances, he totalled nearly 600 runs and 41 wickets; five times he took the important wicket of W. G. Grace in these encounters. Apart from the latter instances, he made other strikes by snatching vital wickets at crucial stages. In the second innings of the Lords encounter of 1881, Barlow bowled and the first three Gents batsmen, namely Grace, Hornby and Lucas, for 27 runs. This was masterly, especially after taking four for 34 in the first knock. His previously mentioned hat-trick three years later was also memorable for the fact that he was captain of the Players that day.

Richard Barlow was a member of Shaw and Shrewsbury's team that toured Australia, via America and New Zealand in 1881-82. Like most of the early touring sides, the players had a rough sea passage, this time from the Irish port of Queenstown to New York. Stopping at San Francisco, a famous baseball pitcher put the tourists out for a very low score, but when odds were laid of twenty crowns to one that Ulyett and Barlow wouldn't put on a century opening partnership in the next innings, the two wily old pro's cleaned up with 166! This same pair were to make England's first Test century opening stand of 122 in the second Test at Sydney, only to be followed by 98 at Melbourne in the fourth Test. Barlow must have gleaned great satisfaction from such deeds after making a 'duck' in his first Test innings. At the end of the tour, lasting eight months, each player received £300 after all expenses were paid, plus the promotors' presentation of a gold medal, which Barlow always wore proudly on his watch chain.

In the early Autumn of 1882 Barlow returned to Australia with Ivor Bligh's side, but this time via the Suez Canal and Ceylon, as it was then known. After viewing the devastation of Alexandria by British battleships, a short stay at Colombo provided welcome relief. Continuing their journey on the 'Peshawar', and just 350 miles out, they were rammed by a ship of 1500 tons. Luckily the liner was able to tow the badly damaged Glen Roy back to Colombo. The impact caused Fred Morley, the Notts fast bowler, to break a rib, an injury that contributed to his early death, soon after arriving back in

England. The voyage eventually ended after seven weeks, and in the sixth game of the tour at Sydney, Barlow's 80 helped to put on 224 for the second wicket against New South Wales. His partner, the Middlesex amateur, G. F. H. Leslie, amassed 144. Barlow's tour highlight came when Australia were set just 153 to win at Sydney in the third Test. From 34 overs, 20 of which were maidens, an analysis of seven for 40 was enough to ensure a 69 run victory for England. A collection of £30 was handed to the match winners, together with gifts of various mementoes and a silver cup. Each player received £220 from the Melbourne Cricket Club, the tour organisers, after the last game.

Richard Barlow's third, and final tour of Australia, was with the Lillywhite, Shaw and Shrewsbury side of 1886–87. The tourists two defeats were both inflicted by New South Wales, with C. T. B. Turner's pace proving unmanageable, and giving him match figures of 13–54 and 14–59 respectively. This southern state really pressed home their two humiliating defeats of the tourists by 'entertaining' them to a mild earthquake at Cootamundra, and a cloud of locusts during a country game at the same location, causing players and spectators to take evasive action by lying on the ground. The New South Wales batsmen were helped when wearing their usual face masks to combat the irritation of flies! With each tour member clearing £320 after expenses, Barlow recalled this being his most enjoyable tour of the three. Richard Barlow's feat of not missing one game of these tours, was attributed mainly to his consistent performances and superb physical fitness. Offers to coach in Queensland and Melbourne were turned down because of his preference to live and play in England.

In 17 Tests, Barlow totalled nearly 600 runs and 35 wickets, but he was a proud man to be selected to open England's batting and bowling in his first home Test of 1882, at the Oval. Although he took five for 19 in Australia's first innings, it wasn't enough to save England's 'demise' and the origin of the 'Ashes'. Richard Barlow played in seven home Tests, with his best returns coming from the game at Manchester, in 1886, to ensure England a four wicket win. In England's first knock he was second highest scorer with 38 not out, followed by the top score of 30 in the second innings. Barlow, under instructions from Hornby to blunt the devastating speed of Spofforth, carried out his orders in style. When Australia were bowled out for 123 in their second innings, Barlow took seven for 44 off 52 overs—revenge, indeed, for '82!

A successful benefit match was played, in 1886, between Lancashire and Notts, at Old Trafford. Over 11,000 people attended on the first day, while the 27,000 overall produced accumulated receipts of

gate money and subscriptions to the tune of £1000. Richard Barlow
played his last county game in 1891 against Yorkshire—who else?
Other counties pressed him for his services after finishing with Lancashire, but there was only one team for Barlow. He even tended the
Old Trafford wicket for 12 months on his retirement, and, for some
years after, stalwart Lancastrians were reminded of Barlow's memory
while watching the antics of Johnny Briggs. It was Barlow, after
seeing Briggs as a fourteen year old play in a benefit game at
Liverpool, who advised the Lancashire committee to take the lad on
to the ground staff. Accepting the shrewd advice, the committee
arranged with Richard Barlow to have Briggs lodge with him. The
youngster must have given his ageing mentor great satisfaction when
the pair played together in the same England and Lancashire teams.
Barlow enjoyed every minute of each game, and, right up to 1914,
and aged 64, he challenged anyone as old, to a single wicket encounter! 'Monkey' Hornby, and other friends, put forward his name as a
first class umpire. It wasn't long after his acceptance that he stood in
Tests, witnessing W. G. Grace's last Test as player and captain, at
Trent Bridge, in 1899. Incidentally, this Test, versus Australia,
marked the debuts of Victor Trumper, J. T. Tyldesly and Wilfred
Rhodes. Barlow's umpiring status was never questioned. Even when
no-balling Northants 'quickie', George Thompson, in the county's
game against the 1907 South Africans, it was accepted without
complaint from the offender.

He died at his Blackpool home in 1919, aged 69, and was buried in
Layton Cemetery close by. He designed his own headstone showing a
set of stumps being broken by a ball, with the inscription 'Bowled at
Last'. Barlow left £1,574 on his death, but his home proved a lasting
mausoleum to his greatness, a veritable museum of cricketania. His
initials were carved over the front door with a stained glass window
in the entrance hall showing Lancashire's three great stars, Barlow,
Hornby and wicket-keeper Pilling. This coloured memento was presented to Richard Barlow by the M.C.C., in recognition of his feats
over the three Australian tours. The same three heroes, plus Lord
Sheffield's cricket ground, are depicted in a tiled floor. Each room
reeked of cricket, with the walls festooned with photographs, gifts
and other mementoes collected while in this country, and abroad.
Even the bathroom wall revealed a line of bats, including one of
Barlow's favourites, a nut brown specimen that had helped him score
over 4,000 of his runs. His writing paper bore a motif of a batsman
with a pointed beard, remarkably similar to his own! Surprisingly,
such a home steeped in examples of cricket's greatest traditions was
called . . . 'Glen Maye'.

CHAPTER THIRTEEN

Gregor Macgregor
(England & Middlesex) 1869–1919

WHILE many squint-eyed marksmen tried to line up the rapid flight of grouse over the purple heather on the twelfth day of August, 1890, hundreds of wide-eyed spectators sat spellbound during England's second Test Match with Australia, at the Oval. It had been one of those odd low scoring games affected by rain, where neither side managed more than a total of 102 in any innings, and with W. G. Grace being dropped first ball in his second knock, he retained his record of never being dismissed for a 'pair' in first class cricket, by the narrowest of margins. To the end it had been 'nip and tuck' with fortunes favouring one team, then the other, but with England needing just 95 to win, and the score standing at 93 for 8, anything could happen. So it was down to England's number nine, Gregor Macgregor, Scotland's rugger international three-quarter back, and her number ten, John Sharpe, a Notts County soccer player, to salvage something from the pending deabacle. Perhaps fortunes favoured England to have two such fleet-footed athletes at the crease, for with the help of a mis-directed throw from J. E. Barrett, the pair scampered home to a narrow victory by two wickets.

Such tight situations were 'grist for the mill' to Gregor Macgregor's resolute character; he thrived on moments when one's determination was a prime factor to win through. He loved that extra air of professionalism and keeness so apparent when Middlesex met rivals like Yorkshire and Surrey, but it was in the Edinburgh suburb of Merchiston, on August 31st, 1869 that this Scottish tenacity first saw the light of day. As a six and seven year old Macgregor loved to play cricket on the lawns of his friends homes, only youngsters knock-abouts, aided by enthusiastic parents, but the nurseries for future stars, nonetheless. His introduction to competitive cricket arrived during his two years at Craigmount School, where in the summer term of 1878 he scored 65 runs and did the hattrick in one match, and topped this with a century in another. From here he moved on to Cargilfield

Gregor Macgregor

Preparatory School, an establishment that was to produce two more test players in A. P. F. Chapman and Jonathon Agnew. The former, of course, was to captain England. Progressing to Uppingham, Gregor Macgregor was one of the forerunners of the many future cricket celebrities produced by that academic establishment. Although Mac, as he was to be affectionately known, had kept wicket at Craigmount, he gained his Uppingham colours as a useful bat and good fielder. Two years in the school eleven proved invaluable experience before being accepted by Jesus College, Cambridge, and his baptism into Varsity cricket.

It is said that when two extremes of personality gel, it is for life. This was certainly borne out when Mac and Sammy Woods first met at Jesus, for Mac, with his quiet unassuming nature and slow speech, was a complete opposite to the Australian's flambuoyant ways. But what exciting times these two were to provide the Varsity games with over the next few years, because both gained their Blues that first Spring of 1888, with Mac's special 'keeping expertise immediately recognised in tandem with Sammy's immense bowling pace. This duo proved a continual threat to Oxford between 1888 and 1891 with Mac standing up to, and effortlessly taking Sammy's expresses. the Hon. Alfred Lyttleton had been the light blues best wicket keeper up to this point in time, but it was generally accepted that the new boy possessed even greater qualities, a fact that A. G. Steel, a respected critic of the game and a personal friend of the honourable gentleman's, agreed with. The two room mates carried on the age-old tradition of entertaining the opposition in their room prior to a match. It was said how meals of cold beer and hot lobster were graciously refused by slightly suspicious opponents who thought it better to abstain in order to be of peak fitness the next day. Never was the food known to waste, for the two generous providers cleared the table with ease, then proceeded to do the same with a bemused enemy on the cricket field on the morrow! Once, during one of these convivial get togethers, Sammy accidentally nudged his stumper through a plate glass window, and later recalled it to be the worst moment of his life, even after seeing his friend emerge miraculously unscathed.

They were heady days indeed, to be at Cambridge University at this time. The strength of Varsity cricket can be measured by looking at the Cambridge side of 1890, captained by Sammy Woods. It's ranks included Digby Jephson, F. S. Jackson and F. G. J. Ford, but Mac was to get acquainted with others he was to meet in future Middlesex sides in which he figured. It is best illustrated by looking at Cambridge's match against Sussex that year at Brighton, when it's first four batsmen had all played for Middlesex and three of them scored centuries in this game. In a total of 703–9, Ford made 191, Mac 131, Foley 117 and the fourth, R. N. Douglas, a mere 62! Such was Mac's success in 1890, with the bat and gloves, that he made his Test Match debut at Lords against Australia, followed, of course by that nail-biter at the Oval. Incidentally, when considering that both games were played on rain affected wickets, the fact of Mac not conceding a single bye remains outstanding. Ten years on, in the England v Australia Test at Lords, Mac and Blackham didn't allow a bye in a total of 618 runs, a remarkable feat even on a good strip. Mac's final game for the University was in 1891 when he skippered the side to a two wicket victory over Oxford. A nice way to end an important phase of his academic and sporting education.

Before leaving the Varsity scene, it would be improper not to mention Mac's memorable deeds on the rugger field. Gaining his Blue in 1889 as a full back, many was the time his safe hands and consistent touch-kicking had rescued the light blues from an Oxford surge. His first of several Scottish caps arrived that season, but he played most internationals as a three-quarter back. Sammy Woods was also to play with him in the University side, but were opponents when Scotland met England. A. E. R. Stoddart, Mac's Middlesex team mate, also played for England at the time, and Sammy, good naturedly pointed out how 'Stoddy' seemed to hold back against Scotland for fear of injuring his county colleague! It was fitting that such close friends as Sammy and Mac should both go down from Cambridge together, but what future battles, with and against each other, were these two to be involved in.

As already stated, Middlesex and Lords were to enjoy the sight of the wicket keeper's art at its best, together with the welcome company of Gregor Macgregor for a number of years to come. At the age of 23 he played the first of his 184 county games at Old Trafford, in July, 1892, and retained his place for the rest of the season. Although his batting technique left a lot to be desired, he watched the ball carefully when playing mostly off the back foot, and with almost 5,000 runs for Middlesex, many were made at important times, even when batting quite low in the order. Most of them came on the leg side, and all of his three first class centuries were made against Sussex. Why Sussex should have had to suffer this indignity by themselves is a mystery, but often other sides felt the fighting qualities of his batting when having the game snatched from them by his dogged persistence. Many more teams, however, were made aware of his wicket-keeping prowess, a feature of his play quite unique. Has there ever been a better amateur 'keeper?

His methods were simple. He was never known to show any histrionics when appealing to the umpire, just a quiet enquiry which batsmen of that era knew full well must be awfully close, because he only bothered with confident requests. With the usual crouched, straddled stance, he stood up to all bowlers, regardless of pace, and his gloves were held fingers down near the off stump. Mac took the ball with his gloves in the same position, whereupon his hands showed no disfigured joints as did his fellow 'keeper's, who chose to take throws and bowling deliveries fingers forward. His gloves were little more than hedging gauntlets, while his pads were almost 'topless', like our modern ones. He did use small pads of chamois leather in his palms to lessen the impact of fast bowling, surely more acceptable to the slip fielders than the smell of Les Ames's beefsteak shock absorbers on hot days, when Harold Larwood was at his fastest! It was common knowledge how he made moderate bowling look good, also many poor throws were to appear reasonable. There seemed little different movement when taking fast or slow bowling, while his expressionless features remained undisturbed. Ranji described them as sphinx-like, and Sammy Woods explained his mate's bland face as almost boring! It was accepted that Lancashire's tiny Richard Pilling was his closest rival for the England spot, and it is interesting to read comparisons with Mac and the Hon. Alfred Lyttleton, when it was said how the latter was more competent when catching because he held his hands further back from the stumps, but this did impede his speed in stumping. Summing up, all agreed that Mac was superb at both phases of 'keeping. His overall first class record more than justifies this conclusion with 411 catches and 148 stumpings.

When A. J. Webbe, aided at times by Mac and Ford, finally gave up the reins of the Middlesex captaincy in 1898, the committee had to look no further than the wicket keeper for a replacement. Mac was not only a brilliant reader of the game in general, but wickets in particular. He knew the type of roller to be used, and most of the leading batsmen's faults. He often advised his bowlers where to bowl for the best method of attack or restraint. Once he told the mercurial Albert Trott that ". . . if he had had a head instead of a turnip, he could be the best bowler in the world!" Such jibes were taken in good part for Mac was a popular and successful skipper. His players recognised that he didn't suffer fools gladly, that his confidence never deflected him from an intended goal, but they did notice how nervous their captain was before batting, though never when 'keeping, and he admitted it!

Success beckoned when starting the 1903 season with seven victories and four draws in the first 12 games, and even after sustaining defeat at Headingly, the accolade of champions was conferred on Middlesex after the final match. Mac carried his victorious side well, but that stocky figure and those swarthy features seemed to glow with suppressed pride, while his coal-black eyes gleamed with a modest serenity. Much credit must go to the captain and his work behind the stumps, but another important factor blossomed the day B. J. T. Bosanquet persuaded his skipper to let him try his 'mystery' ball, later to be known as the 'googly'. Immediately batsmen had problems with it, and Middlesex were on the way. So the county had, at last, pulled off the championship for the first time.

Gregor Macgregor's stint as captain was not all plain sailing, for at the time he took the post Surrey were refusing to play Middlesex over an issue of Sir Timothy O'Brien's unwise decision to use bad language to a Surrey official. Tricky negotiations followed, wherein Mac utilised his friendly temperament and tactful recommendations expertly. The retirement of Sir Timothy helped enormously to put the relationship between the two counties back on an even keel. Not all of Mac's little ruses worked out on the field of play, as shown when Gilbert Jessop was expected at Lords in the Gloucestershire v Middlesex clash of 1990. Jessop's dashing ways with the bat were most popular with the doting public, but not so endearing to opposing skippers whose job it was to dismiss him early, or more difficult still, to improvise a plan of containment. It came to Mac's notice that a day or two before the match a leg-break bowler named Williams had defeated Gilbert Jessop early on in a country game, so the call went out for the victorious bowler to try and repeat his success at Lords. He did play, but Jessop made a debut century at headquarters, followed by 58 not out in the second knock when Gloucestershire cruised to a five wicket win. It proved to be just another game on another day for the unlucky Williams, but he did go on to play 27 games for Middlesex.

Probably Mac's outstanding performance for the county was at Nottingham, in 1902, when he caught one and stumped five batsmen in the second innings. Four of them, including William Gunn, were off Bosanquet's bowling, while Arthur Shrewsbury was lured from his ground by Wells. Mac's useful knock of 39 helped set up a nine wicket Middlesex victory. By the year 1907 Mac was finding it difficult to play regularly because of his vocation as a City stockbroker, so when the county met Kent at Tonbridg that year, he decided to call it a day, but was that decision too hasty? The wicket was always unpredictable, but he still didn't concede a bye in Kent's innings defeat, and managed to catch six and stump one! When Mac was absent because of business commitments, Harry Murrell took over the gloves, a job he made permanent upon Mac's retirement. The captaincy went to 'Plum' Warner, who thought his predecessor a hard act to follow.

Gaps in the county fixture lists of this era enabled players to turn out for top club sides, and how grateful Hampstead C.C. must have been when Mac offerd to join A. E. Stoddart and Australia's 'Demon' Spofforth in its ranks. He also played for his old boys side, Uppingham Rovers. In 1905 Mac added the distinction of representing Scotland at cricket to his rugger honours. Between 1890 and 1906 Gregor Macgregor played for the Gents 14 times, and such was their batting strength during the mid 1890's that Mac was generally down at number 11. Surely his catching of Lancashire's Frank Sugg, in the 1893 match at Lords, must remain a highlight of such an illustrious career. Standing up to Kortright's extreme pace he took the catch low down on the off side, and the fact he let through no byes in the match seemed quite insignificant. As the Gents skipper in 1901 Mac had seen Sir Pelham Warner make his debut as an opener for the Amateurs, while six years later Mac was the opposing captain when the youthful Jack Hobbs opened for the Professionals at Lords. Although neither did himself justice on these two auspicious occasions, both were to play important roles in the game's future evolution. Upon his retirement Mac's successor to the 'keeper's gloves for England was Arthur Lilley, and it's a statistical freak to see that their records for the Gents and Players respectively, are identical: 38 victims (31 caught and 7 stumped). Gregor Macgregor toured Australia with Lord Sheffield's side in 1891–92, but was a surprising disappointment to the Australian fans. Towards the end of his playing days he was a member of the M.C.C. touring party to North America, in 1907.

Middlesex C.C.C. and England cricket were served faithfully by Mac as an honorary treasurer to the former, and as a selector to the latter. He held the treasurer's post at the time of his sudden death in a Marylebone nursing home on August 20, 1919, just a few days short of his 50th birthday. Shortly before this sad day he had attended the Gents v Players match at Lords, and seemed very much himself. His friends were shocked beyond belief at the tragic news, but memories lingered. . . how he rubbed his cheeks with the back of his wicket-keeping gloves while changing ends between the overs. . . and that ever present light blue Cambridge cap worn in the early days. . . such vignettes never fade.

CHAPTER FOURTEEN

E. Lockwood
(Yorkshire) 1845–1921

LASCELLES Hall used to be a small village three miles from Huddersfield, an insignificant backwater of industrial England noted for its few inhabitants working as dedicated weavers at their cottage hand looms. This tiny community will always be remembered for producing the nucleus of early Yorkshire cricket teams, for if Hambledon was 'the cradle of cricket', Lascelles Hall was the celebrated nursery for the county, producing no less than twenty one players. All youngsters were expected to help operate the looms at an early age, but, just as importantly, they received strict tutoring on the cricket pitch, situated in a picturesque setting atop a hill. Most played bare-foot, and with little education available, all their spare time at mid-day and evening was occupied by systematic practice. Each player bowled forty balls, with all batsmen receiving the same, and at the change of wickets, fielders moved round to new positions—catches were thrown while waiting. Any batsman managing to face more than his share of forty balls was fined one penny! Naturally, in such a close-knit settlement, most families were related through marriage, and names such as Bates, Eastwood and Thewliss were household names in Yorkshire county cricket. Indeed it was said that many Lascelles Hall men based their style on John Thewliss, making them easy to recognise. Into such cricket mania was born Ephraim Lockwood, on 4th April, 1845.

The eldest of four children, he fended for himself until the age of 13, but like scores of the other young villagers, he progressed through the practice routines a touch quicker than most, for he showed a rare gift for batting—a talent to keep him as one of England's top batsmen for a period of fifteen years. Lascelles Hall was strong enough to play and beat the Yorkshire side, also Harry Jupp's XI, which was virtually the full Surrey team, while a victory by six runs over the All England XI, in 1867, was outstanding. Ephraim's first real break came with an invitation to play at Lords for the Colts of England, at

From a photo by Albert Sachs, Bradford

E. Lockwood

the start of the 1868 season. The traumatic experience of travelling so far from home may have been reason enough for his failure with the bat, but an even more exciting call was close at hand. It was an August weekend, that same year, when the Yorkshire side travelled down to play Surrey at the Oval, starting on the Monday. After a bus accident at Derby, Yorkshire lost the services of George Freeman and Luke Greenwood, so after a hurried consultation involving Tom Emmett and John Thewliss, it was decided to send for the latter's nephew—Ephraim Lockwood. The wide-eyed recruit arrived at the ground with his playing clothes wrapped in an old newspaper, and how the Oval crowd laughed at the small, undernourished appearance of Ephraim in his tight trousers and a shirt of red, green and black squares.

After shooting out Surrey for 195, Uncle John Thewliss took Ephraim in to open the Yorkshire innings. Slowly, derision was replaced by respect as they put on 176 for the first wicket. The youngster's wicket was the first to fall with his score at 91, while John went on to 108, and final total sufficient to force a victory by an innings and 142 runs. The crowd had really taken the level-headed youngster to their hearts, and as he left the wicket, they scampered to form a tunnel to get a closer look. One cockney passed the remark that "he looked fitter to eat a penny cake than play cricket!" While the Reverend R. S. Holmes, a chronicler of yearly Yorkshire cricket, described him that day as ". . . looking all over an annointed clodhopper". That initial burst of leg-pulling to tease Ephraim must have caused John Thewliss to remember his debut for the county, for those hard bitten Tykes roared for him to take off his jacket when batting—he daren't because of the holes in his shirt. Young Lockwood's success was questioned by the illustrious England and Middlesex batsman, I. D. Walker, when he put forward the argument that if the Surrey fast bowler, Southerton, had been playing, it would have been a different story. Perhaps Ephraim answered this criticism the following year in the same fixture, and in the presence of the notorious bowler, with scores of 103 and 34 not out. There was no denying the debutant's superb performance, but the following Saturday a lob bowler bowled him round his legs for a duck, in a club match—it's a cruel game!

Ephraim Lockwood was only of average height and weight, and his broad shoulders, and feet to match, didn't help to make him a natural athlete. Indeed one lady onlooker suggested that he would run faster given smaller boots! He was, however, blessed with a good eye. His favourite scoring shot was the cut, both fine and square; a powerful stroke he relished to balls even on the middle stump. Opposition skippers went to the trouble of positioning two or three men to combat this shot, but Ephraim's placing was uncanny. He showed great defence on rough wickets by using the straightest of bats, and the patience of Job, but slow bowlers were frequently greeted with lofted drives over their heads. Even before the turn of the century, batsmen tended to leave balls outside the off stump, much to Ephraim's anger, for he often passed the comment "I would have given two shillings a dozen for them!"

Like many folk of the same simple upbringing, Ephraim was rather slow on the uptake, and was made the butt of playful, sometimes cruel, ruses. He resented this when young, but in retrospect accepted it as a part of growing up. Another of life's little annoyances was bestowed upon him in the form of a nickname. In a match between a United North XI and a local Leeds XXII, George Freeman, Yorkshire's very handsome fast bowler, called to Ephraim at point after a skudding shot in that direction. "Look alive, Old Mary Ann"—and it stuck. As the years progressed cricketing colleagues shortened this to "Old Mary". Even with all that chaffing Ephraim remained the quietly unassuming individual that he had always been. Old Ebor, when interviewing the Yorkshire star for a chapter of his book 'Old English Cricketers', remarked how difficult it was to get Ephraim to talk about himself. When asked for his experiences the author was met by the modest response, "nay, I have nowt to say", but after several cagey approaches he had more success. This good natured soul was happily married to Fuller Pilch's niece, who, on Ephraim's admission, knew more about cricket than he did!

'Old Mary' played for many of the top club sides around Huddersfield, because county and other top class games were not as numerous in that period as they are now. His popularity as a professional with Yorkshire was unbounded, and, inevitably, the skipper's job was offered to him. He took over the post from J. Rowbotham in 1876, and held it until succeeded by Tom Emmett in 1878. Such was the laxity in the ranks of the county side that none of these easy going captains were able to control their fellow team-mates. Although Ephraim didn't possess that strong personality needed for leadership, as shown later by Martin Hawke in 1883, there is no denying that he was Yorkshire's leading batsman until the emergence of George Ulyett. He made nearly 8,000 runs for the county, containing six centuries, and 37 knocks of 50 plus. These figures are not great compared with those of present day, but considering the number of games and the roughness of the wickets, this record is a bit special.

Of Ephraim's numerous outstanding innings for Yorkshire, two involved records. His stand with John Thewliss at the Oval, remained a first wicket record until 1897, when Brown and Tunnicliffe set a new one of 378 v Sussex, at Sheffield. The second occurred during a remarkable game against Kent, at Gravesend in 1883. Ephraim, Wisden states, went in just before lunch and was dismissed around six o'clock for 208 out of 297 runs scored while he was at the wicket. Kent then made just 148 and 150, to lose by an innings and 94 runs. This was the highest individual score made by a Yorkshire batsman until Robert Peel's 210, in 1896. 'Old Mary' summed up his performance afterwards with these unaffected words. "Self praise is no recommendation; all the same I may be allowed to say that it was the finest innings I ever saw!" Sadly, such a burst of fast scoring at Gravesend signalled an anti-climax, for a sudden loss of form caused him to be dropped by Yorkshire—the venue proved an ill omen. When asked by Old Ebor which knock gave him the most pleasure, Ephraim recalled his 73 against Lancashire, at Bramall Lane in 1881. His features lit up when remembering 'Monkey' Hornby's vain attempt to plug the gaps on the off side, so easily found by Ephraim's penetrating shots.

The Oval always remained his favourite ground because the 'peculiar light' seemed to agree with him: both facts, surely, being quite unique for a Northern batsman. Following his first two years, he made 67 not out for the North in 1871, 121 against Surrey in three hours without giving a chance in 1872, and 67 not out and 48 for the Players in 1874. Then came 78 against Surrey in 1876, 97 and 20 for the Players in 1877, 62 for the Players in 1881, and 50 versus Surrey in 1882, Such reams of figures tend to be dull, in my opinion, but in this case they aptly illustrate Ephraim's insatiable appetite to play at the Oval. The Gents v Players game at the same ground, in 1873, saw him make a pair, much to W. G. Grace's amusement, (for he caught him off Buchanan's bowling in the first innings, and caught and bowled him in the second). This was the year he missed a lot of cricket through slight sunstroke, perhaps that explained the hiccup! An outstanding summer for Ephraim was the dull, damp one of 1877, when he and W. G. Grace were the only two batsmen to make a thousand runs. Rain again played an important part in Ephraim's benefit match when Yorkshire played Lancashire at Sheffield, in 1882. The weather greatly restricted play, not to mention the takings, and the beneficiary's £591 should have been considerably more.

Ephraim Lockwood first represented the Players in 1869, and, until 1883, played for them another 27 times. Of his total of nearly 1,200 runs, many knocks were completed in rapid time, also showing that he contributed most of the runs while at the wicket. In the Players' only innings of 180, in 1871, he made 76, while his superb innings of 67 not out at the Oval in 1874 made him the first batsman to achieve the distinction of carrying his bat since the fixture was initiated in 1806. During the Lords game, the following week, Allan Hill, his fellow player and villager, completed a hat-trick, again the first time it has been accomplished in the fixture. At Lords, in 1875, Ephraim scored 67 out of the Players' second innings of 165, while the next year, at Princes, he slammed 70 of the Players' first innings of 158. Towards the end of his career he tended to bat in the middle of the order.

Little is mentioned of his high actioned, round-arm bowling, but the mere fact that he took 141 wickets for Yorkshire proves he was useful. He once bowled, unchanged, through both innings of the United North's game with the United South at Bishops Stortford, in 1872. Possibly his most notable county contribution was in the Notts match at Trent Bridge in 1870, when his slow-medium cutters took Nottingham's last wicket, in a last over victory. It so happened that he had bowled the previous over, and taken a wicket, but skipper Iddison didn't have the confidence to let the sometimes wayward Tom Emmett bowl the last. This strange procedure was allowed at that time.

Being born of country stock, it was not surprising that Ephraim loved a tankard of ale, though never to the point of over indulgence, but his aversion to water, especially sea-water, was probably the main reason for him not accepting several invitations to tour Australia. Both Gregory and Spofforth told of the Australian public's disappointment upon 'Old Mary' refusing tours during the 1870's because of his poor attempts to become a sailor, together with his being a sufferer of niggling rheumatism. The Aussies rated him second only to W. G. Grace, which is surprising after his four ducks during two matches against the tourists, played in one week in the year 1882: perhaps they saw enough of him on other occasions. Ephraim's dread of a sea voyage can be gauged by his precautions when simply taking a dip at the sea-side. Lord Hawke recalls in his book 'Recollections and Reminiscences' how, on a visit to Scarborough, Ephraim went out to bathe with a stout rope looped around his chest, and tethered securely to a bathing hut. After lathering himself with soap, and a few quick bobs to rinse it off, the reluctant bather soon retired to the safety of dry land!

When Richard Daft named his team to tour North America in the autumn of 1879, the inclusion of Ephraim's name must have caused a minor shock wave through the cricket fraternity. It was never revealed how the tour captain managed to influence 'Old Mary' to accept, but the matter must have had reservations about his decision, after a terribly rough, seven day crossing from Liverpool to Canada.

George Pinder, Yorkshire's 'keeper, was a constant companion to Ephraim, and it pleased the other members of the party to see the couple's constant mode of walking, one a few yards in front of the other, and both holding a normal conversation. When the party stood gazing at the awesome Niagara Falls, Pinder asked his companion for his thoughts. Quite unperturbed, Ephraim drawled "Nowt at all. If this is Niagara, give me Sheffield any day!" Tom Emmett's version substituted Lascelles Hall in place of Sheffield. Not to be outdone by the air of unconcern, Pinder enquired if his friend wasn't inspired by the millions of gallons of water crashing over the edge. "I see nowt to stop it!" replied the un-impressed Ephraim.

Ephraim Lockwood often remarked of the wish to be home as soon as possible, and, probably, never more so than when the touring team was plagued by swarms of mosquitoes in America. Few of the tourists escaped, but Ephraim suffered more than anyone, with his featuers grotesquely distorted. His case was so bad that when a team photograph was taken at Philadelphia, he had to sit askew to enable the photographer to catch his better side! It was during this period of acute discomfort that he had a run of scores, 0, 0, 10, 0, 0, but soon after, a welcome 60 and 88 in Philadelphia helped to put him near the top of the tour averages. Ephraim's usual air of rustic naivety was put to the test at a Sunday morning church service, when his colleagues were interested to watch his reaction when the offering plate was imminent. An instant 'deep sleep' sufficed until the danger had passed!

When Yorkshire decided to dispose of the services of Ephraim after just six games in 1884, many thought the decision too hasty. To study his record of one double century, seven centuries, 57 occasions when he passed the half century, and in three seasons he exceeded 1,000 runs, perhaps there were grounds for such doubt. The thought of playing elsewhere than his beloved Yorkshire was never entertained, so Ephraim announced his retirement immediately. He actually played once more for his county, admittedly in a less important game, against the Gentlemen of Scotland, at Edinburgh in 1888—he scored 32 in Yorkshire's only innings. Lack of exercise caused Ephraim to grow more rotund, but the taking of a sports shop, or athletic outfitters, as it was then called, helped him to keep in contact with his sporting friends.

Ephraim Lockwood died at Huddersfield on December 19, 1921 at the age of 76, and the county had lost one of its most popular professionals. Cricket had lost a leading star of his day, but its public never forgot him.

CHAPTER FIFTEEN

A. N. Hornby
(England & Lancashire) 1847–1925

IT was when Lord Hawke took over the captaincy of Yorkshire in the last quarter of the nineteenth century that the county was transformed into a well disciplined, smartly turned out unit, a team that was to be county champions and a forerunner of future title winners. Similarly, when Lancashire handed the reins to A. N. Hornby in 1880, this martinet transformed a mediocre county side into one that challenged its rival from over the border, for title honours in the years to come. The friendly rivalry between the two captains was never questioned. Even when Lord Hawke emerged from a bad 'trot' with 126 against Somerset, at Taunton, Hornby was one of many friends who sent a telegram of congratulations to the relieved batsman. Imagine a skipper making such a gesture to his opposite number to-day!

Hornby was born at Blackburn in 1847, into a family that represented the more affluent section of Lancashire social life. His father regularly followed the hounds, and the cricketing son was to follow his example of riding as straight a course over the countryside as the next man. Neville Cardus was to describe the county skipper as ". . . the squire of Lancashire cricket." Upon going up to Harrow, in 1862, it wasn't long before Hornby's cricketing potential blossomed into quite an outstanding talent. He represented Harrow against Eton in 1864, and it was said that the seventeen year old weighed little more than six stones—including his bat! Such a weight deficiency, and a height of barely five feet, was fortunate as he was carried off shoulder high, after a match-winning innings. After another appearance for the school in 1865, and acquiring the nickname of 'Monkey' because of his size and puckish humour, Hornby went up to Oxford and was faced with an important decision. Although his cricket credentials were impeccable, he didn't measure up to certain academic requirements needed to study at such a university, so decided to return home to the family milling business at Blackburn.

R. Pilling, Watson, A. N. Hornby, Barlow

It was after A. N. Horby and three brothers had played for the Gentlemen of Cheshire against the Gentlemen of Lancashire that he and E.K. were asked to play in the Lancashire Gents side versus the Gentlemen of Yorkshire. Shortly after, in 1867, came his first outing with the Lancashire county side, but not until two years later was he to be a regular player. Before making his place permanent, Hornby had the pleasure of playing against the very first touring team from Australia, in 1868. The novelty alone of meeting the players was exciting, but the fact of them being Aboriginals made the occasion one of special significance. Hornby represented East Lancashire against the eleven black players with names like Bullocky, Twopenny, Red Cap, Tiger, King Cole and Dick-a-Dick. At the end of play these unique personalities entertained the onlookers with demonstrations of throwing spears and boomerangs. Young 'Monkey' must have been enthralled, along with the English cricket public, to watch such natural expertise—he left quite an impression himself by scoring 117!

Hornby attained the height of 5' 9½", and weighed 11½ stones, but into this smallish frame he packed enough punch to make everyone aware of his keen spirit, and a desire to make Lancashire a top championship potential. His military appearance, with hair parted in the middle and a neatly trimmed moustache, soon was seen to effect on all leading grounds of England, while his sportsmanlike will to win, and dashing style made him a favourite everywhere. After a smart, upright walk to the wicket, Hornby made runs with an array of punishing shots off the front foot. He was never a 'slogger', but, with an unusually good eye, runs came quickly. this is not to say he couldn't defend, because if the cause called for dour defence, he was competent enough—luckily, this was seldom the case. Never has there been such a run-stealer. Richard Barlow, his Lancashire opening partner, was often the victim of a bad call, but used to be recompensed with a gold sovereign. Once Hornby ran W.G. ragged with short singles, but when the great man was almost run out, Hornby was told that was enough! 'Monkey' was seldom a victim of his own indiscretion, or anyone elses, for on the occasion when George Yates played a shot and called for 'one', he reached the other end to be faced by an unmoved Hornby, and a blunt enquiry. "What the hell are you doing down here, Yates?" Some bowlers lamented when Hornby was out early, for it meant they had to bowl out the rest! It was 'Monkey's' contention in latter life, that more runs were lost than were ever made in a cricket match. As a fielder A. N. Hornby excelled at cover-point or long leg, but was ambidextrous when bowling his cricket assortment. Once, for Harrow Wanderers, he started an over with fast right hand, and completed it with his left!

It was inevitable that such a fine cricketer, and universally liked character would become captain, which he did, in 1880. The players, pro's and amateurs alike, responded wholeheartedly, because they recognised a champion of their cause; someone they had confidence in, and to play their hearts out for. Hornby tolerated nonsense from nobody. Even to the point of putting a fielder in a position he wasn't happy with. Archie MacLaren, fresh up from Harrow, stated his preference for anywhere except point—Archie spent the best part of the match there! Hornby was a tyrant for pre-play practice, as Paul and Hallows found out when the skipper asked them to open the innings, knowing they had been in the bar. The 'culprits' put on 250 for the first wicket. Such brilliance was rewarded by the offer of a drink from their skipper, and both, rather hesitantly, asked for lemonade. Two bottles of ale followed! Another time Hornby questioned Briggs about his sobriety, whereupon the impish bowler ordered the irate captain to the window, to watch his display of trick-cycling— Briggs might have found the task impossible if sober!

A. N. Hornby's example of sportsmanship was exemplary. Apart from making gifts to Barlow of a sovereign after running him out, Hornby gave the same reward to Bird of Warwickshire, after dismissing the Lancastrian with a fine boundary catch. In 1885, Derbyshire followed on and set Lancashire 158 to win, but after the latter were bowled out for 84, with five minutes to spare, 'Monkey' sent a crate of champagne to the winners' dressing room. It was a sad day in the Lancashire versus Gloucestershire match at Old Trafford, in 1884, when Hornby had to inform the Grace brothers, W.G. and E.M., that a telegram had arrived telling of their mother's death. The Lancashire captain abandoned the game to enable the boys to return home to Gloucester. Hornby, whenever possible, liked to bridge the gap between professional and amateur cricketers with minimal actions. When taking the field it was his policy to join the pro's quickly after leaving their separate pavilion gates. He would often call at Old Trafford through the winter months, to see if his pro's were being looked after properly.

These deeds of affection could never distract from his driving demands for each player to give his all for the county. 'Monkey' was known to rebuke his own 'keeper for appealing too much, and he never flinched when standing up to the dominating nature of that intrepid pair, W.G. and E. M. Grace. Hornby was never afraid to experiment. Like the time when skippering the North against the South, at Lords, he asked the Yorkshire 'keeper Pinder if he could keep without a long-stop. This outlandish request was accepted by the game wicket-keeper, who let through only four byes. Such a fine display marked the first time such a field setting had been tried. Archie MacLaren, a prominent captain in latter years, was much influenced by his predecessor's actions. Incidentally, Archie's attractive upright stance was probably the result of Hornby's advice to him as a young player. "Keep your shoulder up and say your prayers". Hornby also knew what acute embarrassement was like when he ordered Crossland to take off his large sweater during a long and successful bowling stint, only for the bowler to point out that he didn't possess a shirt to wear underneath. In the first two years of Hornby's captaincy, Lancashire lost only one game out of 24. His reign lasted until 1891, but in 1897 and 1899 he was asked to come back and lead again at the age of 50. At the Committee's request he shared the job with Crosfield in 1892 and 1893. During these busy years Lancashire won the title in 1881, 1897, and shared it in 1882 and 1899. Albert Neilson Hornby was worth his place for such aggressive, but fair, captaincy; a task he mastered with a natural awareness, together with a tactical mind, and seldom bettered. Lancashire were fortunate indeed to possess such a leader at this time, but his batting caused people to travel long distances to watch. W. G. Grace was the leading batsman, of course, but 'Monkey' was in the top bracket, and actually demoted W.G. to second place, in the first class averages in 1881. That year Hornby was the only batsman to make 1,000 runs, and he achieved his highest ever score of 188 against Derbyshire, at Manchester; he made a mere 145 in the return match. What a year he had, and Lancashire were county champions at the end. It was the general opinion of old scribes that his 161 made at Liverpool, in the 1886 game with Surrey, was the greatest innings he ever played. Remarkably Hornby was the only Lancashire player to make a century between 1870 and 1881—seven in fact! During his 33 years service for the county, and 286 games, 'Monkey' made over 10,000 runs, including ten centuries, and topped its batting averages from 1869 to 1872 inclusive.

Examples of Hornby's rapid scoring rate are numerous, but the following will adequately illustrate his crowd pulling powers, because the game never died when the Lancashire skipper was at the crease. After Yorkshire had set Lancs 148 to win, at Manchester in 1875, openers Hornby and Barlow knocked them off with respective personal scores of 78 not out and 50 not out. The following year the Nottinghamshire scoreboard showed Lancs first wicket falling at 45, with Hornby out for 44 and Barlow not out 0! Lancashire were shot out for 64 by the Kent bowlers at Canterbury, in 1880, but not before Hornby had made a half century. Three years later, at Manchester, Kent again had Lancashire struggling with an enforced follow on, but

'Monkey' followed a first innings 88 with a superbly made 96—Lancashire won by 70 runs! As previously mentioned Hornby could use dour methods when the occasion arose. Such a day was the 27th May when the M.C.C. and Ground met the touring Australians of 1878 at Lords, for no fewer than 31 wickets fell for 105 runs. The M.C.C. batted first and totalled 33, including six ducks, but after the Australians could only muster 41, there was a possible glimmer of hope if the home side could make a reasonable score on a quagmire of a wicket. This was not to be, because after seven more ducks, a total of just 19 left the Australians to make only 12 to win, which they achieved quite comfortably. The nine wicket victory was set up by Spofforth and Boyle with match figures of 1–20 and 9–17 respectively. Hornby's 19 in the first innings was the highest individual score of the match, but he had to retire hurt in the second knock after a shattering blow from one of Spofforth's fastest deliveries. Seeing the plight of his team, 'Monkey' was soon back at the crease to resume hostilities. Even in such a hopeless position he would never capitulate, for it has been stated that after receiving such a sickening blow, many batsmen would not have been able to continue at all.

Unfortunately, but also understandably, Hornby's ebullient nature was the cause of controversial hiccups, when he stood four-square behind his players and his principles. When Lord Harris of Kent questioned the dubious bowling action of Crossland, Hornby backed the bowler to the end. Other counties sided with Kent, but nothing altered 'Monkey's' beliefs. He actually took his players off at the Oval one day, when Crossland's action was barracked. He wasn't averse to using his fighting attributes, as the reporter who had questioned Hornby's tactics in print found out, after being chased half way round Old Trafford. Riotous behaviour broke out at Manchester in 1878, when Gloucester's three Grace brothers were expected. Inadequate seating for the crowd of 17,000 to watch these stars helped to ignite a tricky situation, but Hornby boxed the ears of a clod thrower, and handed him over to the police.

'Monkey' Hornby went on the celebrated tour to North America in 1872, a tour ably organised by the Secretary of the Marylebone Cricket Club, Mr. Fitzgerald. This popular excursion was described in the latter gentleman's book, "Wickets in the West". The tourists proved far superior to ther inexperienced opposition, but the Englishmen were astounded by the number of ladies that attended the matches, not to mention a banquet with cuts off a leg of bear top of the menu! Hornby was a real favourite, as shown by a verse taken from a song, "The Gentlemen Cricketers", and dedicated to the touring team:

"Here's to Hornby who bears the cognomen of 'Monkey',
All muscle and never never feeble or funky;
For pluck skill and strength he is hard to be beaten
By picked men from Winchester, Harrow and Eton!"

In 1878-9 Hornby was a member of Lord Harris' team to Australia, where he topped the averages with 33 for all matches. This amateur side, plus two professionals in George Ulyett and Tom Emmett, experienced a touchy situation in the return match with New South Wales at Sydney. When the state side followed on and Billy Murdock was adjudged run out, the crowd encroached on the playing area with the intention of making trouble. Lord Harris was struck with a stick, but the assailant was grabbed by Hornby and carried to a waiting policeman. 'Monkey's' shirt hung in tatters, but the safety of his skipper was paramount. C. A. Absolom of Kent and Hornby worried the Australian onlookers by never wearing hats in the endless sunshine, but the crowd didn't seem to be aware that the Lancastrian was never seen in a hat of any sort.

Surprisingly, A. N. Hornby was not impressive in Test matches, and even when skippering his country in 1882, at the Oval, his reasoning in holding back C. T. Studd to number 10 was baffling to say the least, especially when losing by just seven runs. He was to captain England again in 1884. If success passed him by at international level, he certainly made up for it in his 31 games for the Gents against the Players. After making his debut in 1869, the first real milestone was in 1872, at the Oval, when he put on 186 for the second wicket with W. G. Grace (W.G. 117, Hornby 80). The next year, at Princes, he made a notable 104 helping the Gents to an innings victory, with W.G. contributing 70, the public were treated royally with yet another partnership. The sight of two such punishing batsmen together must have been well worth seeing. W.G.'s last six scores in this fixture, leading up to the game at Princes, had been 217, 77, 112, 117, 163 and 158! Hornby's monumental knock of 144 in 1877, at the Oval, was another highlight. Hornby, in 1880, again at the Oval, could not prevent the Players from winning by 37 runs, but he made a stubborn bid for a Gents win. Set 173 to win, none of the first five Gents batsmen could reach 10, and after Hornby's 71 the next highest was 14! 'Monkey' Hornby's name will always be remembered when this fixture is mentioned, but his quip when tall William Gunn leaned backwards over the Oval boundary rail in 1881, to catch him, will endure for all time. A fielder commiserated with the outgoing batsman upon his bad luck, but was stopped short when 'Monkey' growled, "Only a damn giraffe could have got near the thing!"

A. N. Hornby had the distinction of captaining England at cricket and rugby, an honour he was to share with A. E. Stoddart, who came later. Hornby played the first of his nine internationals at the age of 30, and was a consistent three quarter or full back. He skippered England in his last match, against Scotland at Manchester, of all places. He declined the offer of the captaincy again at a later date, but was pleased to look back on his five representative games for the North versus the South. I have written of his riding prowess on the hunting field, but his all-round sporting achievement included hurdling at athletic venues, and being a member of the Blackburn Rovers soccer team when they played their first game at the Meadows ground. Lord Harris, in his book, "A Few Short Runs", recalls how 'Monkey' Hornby had the opportunity to put the gloves on and spar with the great Jem Mace, while touring in Australia. Now Hornby could, as we know, look after himself very well, and would never turn down the challenge of a booth bruiser, but Jem, good naturedly, evaded every punch thrown.

After playing his last county game in 1899, A. N. Hornby devoted his retirement to working tirelessly for Lancashire C.C.C. and cricket in general, for apart from being an M.C.C. Committee member, and a J.P., he was an active Lancs President from 1894 to 1916. It was Hornby who brought the Rev. Vernon Royle to Lancashire's ranks, after playing against him when a schoolboy, and before the latter went up to Oxford. 'Monkey' Hornby suffered the traumas of losing two of his four sons in the First World War, and only A.H. was to make the grade as a cricketer. He made his father a proud man by becoming county skipper after Archie MacLaren. Faithful followers looked on nostalgically as the younger's punishing play reminded them of his father—so they named him 'Young Monkey'! One day the onlookers didn't agree with 'Young Monkey's' strategy and showed it by outspoken advice. This ugly scene was quelled when 'Monkey' senior held up the game and went to discuss the crowd's problems with the main offenders: sanity was soon restored. Hornby had always kept a close contact with the watching public, it seems, for he so scattered the crowds one day in his exhuberance when chasing a ball, that one gentleman was quite badly injured, and boundaries were set from then on. A. N. Hornby was always a players' captain, a man who had stood by his colleagues when the laws of the game had been questioned, but he never travelled without a current copy of Wisden's in his bag—just for reference!

Upon his death, at Parkfield, Nantwich in 1925, Lancashire and cricket lost a faithful servant, someone who had been loyal to their cause, even if sometimes in an arrogant fashion, but always for the good of the game. I think the following story sums up 'Monkey' Hornby's standing in cricket, and life in general. Upon taking a three week holiday in Scotland with his family, he left instructions at Old Trafford to send a full report at the end of play each day, together with any available press cuttings, because a personal friend was going to play in the forthcoming games there. These orders, of course, were duly programmed, but at the end of the first week Hornby turned up at the ground to watch for himself; a little matter of 600 miles, including the return journey. Such qualities of sincerity and dedication were held in high esteem, but . . . that was 'Monkey' Hornby.

CHAPTER SIXTEEN

D. L. A. Jephson
(Surrey) 1871–1926

At the dawn of the twentieth century Surrey experienced a difficult rebuilding period, which made life awkward for their new skipper, Digby Jephson. Ever popular with everyone connected with cricket, Jephson took over the role from K. J. Key in 1900, but with his friendly nature and innocent personality he found the going hard, especially in the wake of the county's heady years of success at the end of the previous century. Indeed, Surrey had won the County Championship nine times in the last thirteen years. Captaining Surrey until 1902, Jephson proved one of the country's leading amateur all-rounders, for he attacked most bowling with a variety of hard hitting strokes, while his bowling formed part of cricket's fascinating history—he bowled underarm 'lobs'.

Jephson was born at Clapham in February 1871, and, shortly after, his parents provided his first cross to bear in the form of three Christian names—Digby Loder Armroid. He learnt the initial rudiments of the game at the local Manor House School before going up to Cambridge University where it was explained how the extra Varsity tuition had rounded off his good cricket technique. He gained his Blue in 1890, but when studying his achievements on the field, the question still remains—how? Digby Jephson played in the next two Varsity games as well, but when one considers how he made only one half century while at University, batted in the lower half of the order in his three representative games (number 11 in one), never bowled a ball and batted in all the matches for a total of 31 runs, the fact that he fielded well hardly improves his cricketing attributes to merit a Blue. Perhaps some light is thrown on the mystery when considering the point that the genial, but unorthodox, Sammy Woods was Cambridge University's skipper in 1890 and '91, for wasn't he himself only at Cambridge for so long because his cricketing genius overshadowed a dismal lack of academic requirements, as his examination results showed. Even if such bizarre explanations, in some small way, can

D. L. A. Jephson

account for Jephson's selection in the first two years, the puzzle remains when remembering that the astutely cricket-wise F. S. Jackson still retained him in 1892!

After playing in his first Surrey fixture in 1891 (not first class), Digby Jephson didn't play regularly until 1897. Indeed, he didn't play again until 1894, and after missing 1895 and '96 he then could see his way clear to turn out more often. If this proved a lean period with regard to county appearances, his time was fully occupied with making massive scores and remarkable wicket-taking feats in top London club cricket. Before reverting to 'lob' bowling, Jephson was a fast bowler with a round-arm slinging action. Using the latter delivery he took five Eastbourne wickets in eight balls for the Crystal Palace Club, in 1888. Five years later, again versus Eastbourne, he scored 261 runs in rapid time. When Seaton were the opponents the previous season, Digby Jephson and Stanley Colman put on 300 for the first wicket, a partnership that was to grow into personal friendship in the future. Stanley Colman, a Surrey man through and through, formed the Wanderers Club in 1881. This team often boasted a few county players in its ranks, and its founder is reputed to have collected teams for each season's fixtures for 56 years. Jephson often played, and bowling his new found 'lobs' he claimed all 10 Chiswick Park wickets, in 1894. The next year Norwood bowlers suffered when he made 301 not out in three and a quarter hours. In 1900 Jephson hammered Tonbridge for 226 in an opening partnership of 349, but the crowning joy in such a feat was the fact that his partner was Stanley Colman. The crafty lob bowler again took all ten wickets when playing for G. E. Bicknell's XI v Streatham, in 1902.

Early Surrey team photographs show digby Jephson's tall willowy figure always smartly dressed, but in some the centre parting of his hair is hidden by a fashionable straw boater. He was a very sensitive person, a person who took failure far too much to heart for his own good. Such an outlook many of his colleagues thought, left his temperament just that fraction depleted to qualify for Test cricket.

In the eyes of Surrey followers their well liked skipper gave them much to laud when crashing his shots to all sides of the wicket. His presence on the scene, albeit briefly, helped to steady the rocking boat, but it was the combination of internal pressures, and the team's lack of success that he was unable to cope with. Of his eleven innings of three figures in first class cricket, nine were for Surrey. He formed a formidable opening partnership with Bobby Abel, the 'Cockney sparrow'. These two put on 364 after Derbyshire had made 325, at the Oval, in 1900, with Jephson scoring his highest score of 213. The following year they put together opening stands of 114 and 109 against Sussex, at Hove, when the Surrey captain finished with 95 and 85. He amassed 1,000 runs in a season for Surrey twice: first in 1900 with 1649, followed by 1385 in 1901. In the Oval game against Middlesex, in 1894, Jephson's dismissal by 'hit wicket' in Surrey's second innings caused much interest, and not a little amusement. With his score still on nought a fast ball from J. T. Rawlin splintered his bat from where a fragment dislodged the leg bail. This injustice, as will be seen, was reversed later in suitable style.

Digby Jephson, when the position called for such tactics, could defend stubbornly with brave disregard of personal injury. To medium and fast bowling he played mainly off the back foot, thus putting him in a minority group who chose this style of batting. The fact that he often wore a glove on his bottom hand only reflected an attitude of challenge to most bowlers, but his undaunted methods of defence are admirably illustrated by Lord Hawke in his book 'Recollections and Reminiscences'. The occasion was Brockwell's benefit match at the Oval, in 1900, when Lockwood and Jephson had accounted for 209 runs of Surrey's total of 360. Taylor and Tunnicliffe did the same for Yorkshire with 248 out of 380. There followed a lot of rain, and when Rhodes and Haig had Surrey on a drying wicket, struggling on 6–31, the eventual county champions looked home and dry. This was Digby Jephson's cue to bat resolutely for over an hour, which deprived Yorkshire of the time needed to knock off the few runs required for victory.

The all round ability of Jephson was a blessing to his county selectors at this period of reshuffling their ranks. Apart from his batting and bowling, not to mention his above average fielding, Surrey were often thankful for his eagerness to keep wicket, when injuries called for a replacement. Bobby Abel used to fill the role of stand-in, but the threat of hand injuries to one of the most consistent run-getters forced the club to look elsewhere for a substitute.

Up until the turn of the century lob bowling had been dominated by Sussex's veteran Walter Humphreys and Jephson, with Worcestershire's G. H. Simpson-Hayward taking over in the early 1900's. Gilbert Jessop admitted to being more at home against the former pair because of their more orthodox methods, while he found the Worcester bowler created more spin on the ball when using this freakish delivery. Digby Jephson's use of subtle leg-spin and flight caused batting stars many embarrasing moments. When bowling his leg break his crouch was more prominent, almost causing him to scrape his hand on the ground, as can be seen in Spy's excellent cartoon. This cramped action inevitably brought him the nickname 'Lobster'! Gilbert Jessop himself suffered one most uncomfortable incident when being left stranded down the wicket, enabling the 'keeper to remove the bails in his own time. To have captured the prized wicket of Jessop for 35 was a memorable feat, but imagine the bowler's amazement when umpire Bob Thoms replaced the bails, mumbling something about disappointing the Saturday crowd with such rubbish, so—'Not Out'! Needless to say Gilbert Jessop registered another century. At Chesterfield, in 1899, Jephson had more luck when taking 5–12 against Derbyshire, while at the Oval in 1904 he played his last game for Surrey, and what more fitting opponents than Middlesex. His 4–57 included a hattrick, with victims Bosanquet, Nicholl and MacGregor giving Digby Jephson the last laugh when remembering the same fixture a decade earlier.

Although the honour of representing his country did not fall to Jephson, it was his good fortune to play for the Gentlemen in the next most prestigious fixture of the cricket calendar. The first of his eleven appearances was in 1894, at the Oval, but not until 1899 did he really make his mark when taking six of the Players' wickets for twenty one runs. The match started at Lords on W. G. Grace's 50th birthday, and fittingly, he made a memorable 78 before being run out. Coming in as a late replacement Digby Jephson demoralised a Players side which batted down to number ten. They just were not able to master his well flighted lobs in an analysis of 18.4 overs, seven maidens and six for 21. Superb fielding helped to bring about the collapse, especially two boundary catches by Archie MacLaren, one of which he took after sprinting thirty yards. W. G. Grace was seen running to the fence to congratulate the catcher. "Well caught, Archie. You caught it finely", the excited doctor shouted in his familiar high pitched voice. It is stated how the crowd roared its appreciation at such a gesture. A cutting from a next morning's newspaper explains how "the member of the pavilion gave Digby Jephson a reception he was not likely to forget". In those halcyon days it was many a captain's ploy to open the bowling with pace at one end and spin at the other. Jephson often opened the Gents' attack with Kortright or Bradley; indeed he had Bobby Abel his Surrey team-mate in all sorts of trouble in 1900, at the Oval, before bowling him for two—much to the crowd's amusement. He did the same the following year, but not until Abel had reached 247! When Lancashire's master bowler, S. F. Barnes, made his Players debut at the Oval in 1902, a defiant Jephson figured in an unbroken partnership of 73 runs in 70 minutes, with Charles McGahey to save the Gents from a certain innings defeat; the result was a draw.

From 1903 digby Jephson's working commitments at the London Stock Exchange made it very difficult for him to wholly justify his presence in the Surrey side, indeed he only played that one game in 1904. Apart from coaching keen young Varsity cricketers at Fenners, most of his time was to be taken up in cricket journalism, when writing regular articles for Wisden and the Westminster Gazette. When editor, Sir Pelham Warner, formed the Cricketer magazine in 1921, Digby Jephson was one of his first columnists. He will be remembered as the author of a book of verse entitled "A Few Overs".

The game lost a valuabale asset upon his untimely death at the age of 54, following a heart attack. In that January of 1926 cricket followers could well have recalled C. B. Fry's reference to Digby Jephson, in the famous 'Book of Cricket'. The apt epitaph would simply have read—"A thorough cricketer".

CHAPTER SEVENTEEN

Charles I. Thornton
(Kent & Middlesex) 1850–1929

THE challenge and thrill to leave the crease and drive any bowler back over his head must be the ultimate for any batsman, in any grade of cricket. This D'Artagnan attitude was always apparent in Charles Thornton's batting, because, in his opinion, it was the only way to play the game. Cricket was to be enjoyed, not only by the player, but the onlooker was entitled to be entertained, and Thornton was probably the most popular 'crowd-pleaser' in the second half of the nineteenth century to implement this theory.

Such a talented son was born to the Reverend W. J. Thornton and his wife on March 20th 1850 at Llanware Vicarage, Hereford. Sadly both mother and father were to pass away when the lad was only five years old. With his brother Henry, Charles was adopted by Archdeacon and Mrs. Harrison, and went to live at Canterbury. Many hours spent playing cricket on the spacious lawns soon helped the aspiring Charles to higher places. His first senior game of cricket was for Great Mongeham, near Ramsgate in 1861, and after making a promising 22 not out, Thornton's friend and tutor was so encouraged that he predicted his prodigy would ". . . gain fame as a cricketer".

Arriving at Eton in 1861 he played very little cricket for the first three years. After this lapse he was invited to practice with Fred Bell, the resident college professional, but after seeing his best deliveries despatched into neighbouring trees, and the misery of having to fetch them each time, the old pro' had bigoted misgivings about his assailant's ability. Although Charles Thornton made the Eton XI in 1866, it was his contention that Fred Bell was the reason he didn't achieve this distinction earlier, in 1865. Thornton played for three years, and although he skippered the Eton side in his last year, 1868, it was never his good fortune to be in a winning side. He did leave his mark by making a half century in each of the three games. It was a healthy Eton appetite that brought the nickname 'Buns', but his run capacity was also maturing, for he made 1,483 runs in 1867. He was affection-

Charles I. Thornton

ately called 'Buns' by his numerous friends to the end of his life span, a name which will remain indelible through cricket's history.

It was the year of his captaincy which produced the initial blast that was to make Charles Thornton the player for people to watch. Although only 19 years of age, he hit a ball from an already suffering Harrow bowler, C. T. Giles, straight over the pavilion at Lords—the old pro and third in line of succession, Lillywhite recalled it to be the biggest straight drive he had witnessed, while Lord Harris, who was batting at the other end described how the two balls before went into the old armoury and over Block D, respectively. The fourth ball never left the ground and bowled him; such was the unpredictable Lords wicket of that era.

Charles Thornton went up to Cambridge in 1868 and, with his cousin, P. M. Thornton, would often travel up to Lords and the Oval to watch the cricket. These excursions occurred during their first two years of residence, for in 1869 Thornton made his cricket debut for the University. He played four seasons, and, as at Eton, he captained the eleven in his last year, 1872. Pleasingly, he was a member of the winning side three times. His impish humour shone through on the day the University side were soon four wickets down for the very few runs. Thornton queried the pitch length, and was proved right. With a new pitch prepared the match was restarted, whereupon his side made lots of runs! Fenners remained one of his favourite grounds, probably because he played there so many times. Perhaps, after all, it was because of the fact that so many of his drives cleared the fences on so many occasions. His strong Cambridge University Cricket Club connections brought him the President's accolade in 1873. As we shall see in his later life, he loved to arrange and manage visiting teams to various parts of the country. For twenty six seasons he took a strong XI back to play the University side at Fenners.

After leaving Cambridge, Thornton found more time to play for Kent, for his previous matches had been played only during vacations. His first game for the county came while he was at Eton. Charles Thornton played only 18 matches for Kent between 1867 and 1872, but he still finished with an average of 29, which was considered good at that time. The Canterbury ground was where fervent Kent supporters witnessed many of his long carrying hits. The longest recorded was made v The M.C.C. in 1871 when Thornton slammed a ball from W. M. Rose into Nackington Road, a carry from hit to pitch of 152 yards, measured by the Kent secretary W. St. Clair Baker. Lord Harris recalled another Canterbury match v M.C.C. in 1869 when Charles Thornton hit four balls from a 4 ball over, "all over the ring". On one occasion, when playing Surrey at Canterbury, he hit a ball perpendicularly to such a height that two runs had been completed before Stephenson, at point, circled the descending ball and misjudged it so badly that it dropped five yards behind him! Possibly it was the mesmeric effect of such a high flying cricket ball, because it happened again at Scarborough when Thornton hit a ball from Tom Emmett to the far boundary. Louis Hall studied the approaching catch and ran in, then back, only for it to drop harmlessly without making contact!

Charles Thornton made his highest score when just 19 years of age. Kent played Sussex on The Common ground, Tunbridge Wells in 1869, and he made 124, including nine sixes. Arthur Haygarth, in Volume XI of his Scores and Biographies, wrote how the ball was hit ". . . far over the canvas with which the ground was enclosed". Had they been run out, he suggests, each one would have been worth eight runs! Perhaps the boundaries were a handicap to Thornton, even when only sixes were recorded. Although Kent lost by an innings to Notts. behind the Angel Hotel, Tonbridge in 1869, Charles Thornton slammed 76 out of 114, in Kent's second innings, and it contained only nine singles.

With business commitments now taking precedence, he found himself in London a lot of the time. Because of the situation it proved more convenient for Thornton to join Middlesex, and made his debut in 1875. He played only 29 games until 1885. It was at Princes ground that he hit the Oxford University bowler, F. M. Buckland out of the ground four times in the over. For such a prodigious hitter he only made five centuries in his relatively short first class career.

Charles Thornton was six feet tall and weighed 13 stones, but, on his own admission, possessed only average sized arms. Being strong in the legs and hips, his power was generated from perfect timing, coupled with natural ability in getting to the pitch of the ball quickly. Such easy movement was gained, Thornton explained, by not using pads or gloves, which only helped to impede his shots. Genial Sammy Woods of Somerset, and some of Thornton's old Varsity friends dispelled such a statement of refusing protection. Woods had seen small, light shin guards under his flannells, while in later life, Thornton did condescend to wear a glove on one hand. Injury, it seemed, was not important as was proved on the occasion when Cambridge University played Charles Thornton's XI. Sammy Woods, one of the fastests bowlers of his time, tore off one of Thornton's finger nails, but the fact of the ball going on to the wicket to bowl him upset the captain more. It made no difference to him whether the bowler was fast or slow—he loved to use his feet to drive, and upon missing the ball, the momentum of the swing enabled him to ground his bat before being stumped. No one has ever hit so far, so high, so often. He hit the ball out of most grounds he played on; no mean feat for someone claiming never to have received any form of coaching. While practising before play in front of the pavilion at Brighton in 1876, he crashed a ball 168 yards, a shot measured by the historian, James Pycroft. Another hit, shortly after, travelled 162 yards. It would appear that a measuring chain was always handy when Thornton batted, because, when playing on the Orleans Club ground at Twickenham in 1878 for an England XI v the Australians, he made a shot that landed 152 yards away, off the bowling of A. F. Boyle. Cricketers A. Rylott and F. Wild did the measuring. Charles Thornton founded the Orleans Club at Twickenham, a club strong enough to hold its own against touring Australians and Oxford University. Thornton is credited with hitting balls out of three sides of the Oval. He once put three in succession over the grandstand, next to the pavilion, but were only registered as four each because they failed to leave the ground!

Although Thornton didn't play a lot of county cricket he did take part in the Gents versus the Players fixture from 1869 to 1875. He always proved a welcome participant with his story telling, and infectious humour. Stories of his hitting are legion, but his prowess as an underarm 'grub' bowler tends to get overlooked. This mode of delivery, perhaps, is surprising for someone so agile in the field, and possessing the strength to throw a cricket ball up to distances of 106 yards. For his own XI versus Kings School, Canterbury in 1870, he bowled down all 10 wickets in an innings. He caused a slight 'scene' at the Oval in 1870, when he bowled the three Surrey favourites Jupp, Humphreys and Pooley. The crowd couldn't stand such humiliation from the young Cambridge University bowler, shouting "Take the . . . off". After Willsher walked to the boundary and pointed out that if they didn't behave, the University would never play there again, good sense prevailed. Another bowling milestone occurred when Charles Thornton bowled for the Gentlemen of the South versus the Players of the South at the Oval in 1871, ending with the figures of 4–38 from 29 overs.

Charles Thornton became chairman of a large timber firm based in Old Broad Street, London, and it was these activities that prevented him from taking part in tours abroad. When on business trips he did play in Ceylon (Sri Lanka), Australia, China, Japan and America, but, sadly, other tours were never accepted. He was once lured by the sum of £3,000 to go to Australia on tour, but declined. Probably the closest he came to touring was as a member of the team to Canada in 1872. In R. A. Fitzgerald's book of that trip, "Wickets In

The West", still a classic of cricket literature, the ups and downs of early touring are admirably described. When it seemed doubtful whether Charles Thornton would accept the invitation, he received a telegram stating "All Canada disappointed if you stay behind. Pray come". It was suggested he made up his mind after reading an article on seasickness, with an accompanying illustration of a sinking ship!

Most of Thornton's cricket life was occupied arranging cricket matches, and managing teams to play at grounds such as Canterbury, Fenners and Scarborough. Perhaps he liked to be captain, plus the added authority to bat at number one! When Thornton and Lord Londesborough arranged two teams to play in the Scarborough Visitors versus Lord Londesborough's XI game in 1871, little did the two captains realise that it was the forerunner to the Scarborough Festival, founded by Thornton in 1875. A week of fixtures including such sides as the M.C.C., the Yorkshire XI, the touring Australians and Gents v Players, lasted over many years. Charles Thornton remembered playing his first game there, on the Castle Hill, when iron bails were used to counteract the strong wind. Inevitably, Scarborough Visitors witnessed several 'Thornton' thunderbolts, but a few weren't even in the ground. During the Gentlemen of England v I. Zingari in 1866, Charles Thornton crashed 107 not out in 70 minutes, including seven sixes, 12 fours and seven singles, in 29 scoring strokes (he was credited with eight sixes, but one was due to overthrows). Two consecutive hits went through the same window, whereupon the batsman suggested leaving the window open! Another, from the bowling of England spinner, A. G. Steel, travelled through the gap between two rows of terraced houses, finally coming to rest in Trafalgar Square. Years later, Thornton loved to tell the tale of when a lady asked him if he was the gentleman who had hit a ball into Trafalgar Square, she quickly followed with the question—"Were you batting at Lords or the Oval?" W. G. Grace once told Thornton that he wouldn't survive an over of brother, E. M.'s lobs. Never ducking a challenge the batsman stated he would hit six new balls out of the ground in three overs. The feat was accomplished in just two overs! It wasn't all 'Rory of the Rovers' material, because he is saddled with the dubious distinction of getting three ducks in a game. He was playing against Oxford University at the Parks, and had a duck by his name when the wicket was considered too dangerous to continue. with a new one prepared, and the match restarted, Thornton achieved a 'pair'.

In 1894, after 25 years of unfailing service to the Scarborough Festival, the Earl of Londesborough presented Charles Thornton with a silver loving cup (valued at 50 guineas), subscribed to by many friends. Later, in 1921, T. L. Taylor, President of Scarborough Cricket Club, conferred the Honorary Freedom of Scarborough upon Charles Thornton, while the very next evening he was presented with his portrait painted by Sir Leslie 'Spy' ·Ward. In later years, as Thornton lost contact with many M.C.C. members, the task of getting together an M.C.C. XI fell to H. D. G. 'Shrimp' Leveson-Gower, who took his first team to the Scarborough Festival in 1899. Much to Leveson-Gower's pleasure, C. I. Thornton happily approved of his name being retained in the fixture list.

During winter months Charles Thornton loved to hunt in the 'foxy' county of Leicestershire, and the Vale of Aylesbury. His cousin, P. M. Thornton (who became Middlesex C.C. Honorary Secretary in 1871), accompanied him on many of these outings. When Thornton's cricketing days ended he was able to spend more time enjoying his other favourite hobbies, criminology and the cinema. Whenever possible he could be found in the front row of the Old Bailey, studying the topical murder case with profound concentration, and Arthur Gilligan, the old Sussex skipper, recalls that on a few occasions he saw him produce a black wallet containing ancient and recent newspaper cuttings describing notable trials. Many a difference was settled by the authentic contents of that black wallet. He was still enjoying his second pasttime up to and during the years which preceeded his death. It was not unusual for him to go to the cinema twice a day, and his knowledge of actors and actresses was prolific.

His undying love of cricket was obvious when he appeared regularly at Lords, the Oval and Brighton to watch the current game. It was almost sacreligious to sit in his favourite front seat in the Lords pavilion, and the Committee room in the pavilion at Brighton was another of his regular haunts. He loved to watch and compare up and coming young players, to assess potential and constructive point out their attributes and failings. Arther Gilligan remembered him watching Wally Hammond closely at the crease, when the great batsman was just a lad. Moving behind the bowlers to get a front view, he returned to the pavilion most enthusiastic about the technique he had just seen, and not since the First World War had anyone impressed him so much. Two years later Wally Hammond played in his first Test Match (Christmas Eve, 1927 at Johannesburg).

The nation, and the game lost one of its most popular brothers when Charles Thornton died in London in 1929, aged 79.

CHAPTER EIGHTEEN

S. M. J. Woods
Australia, England & Somerset (1867–1931)

THE five brothers Woods travelled each day to Sydney's Royston College on a steamer that plied from Manly Beach across the harbour. Such healthy boys, of course, were keen to play most sports, and, on each trip all gained special boxing tuition from one of the large coloured deck hands, between his usual chores of rope hauling. Smiling easily the negro would kneel on one knee as each aspiring pugilist tried his hardest to land a blow. These brothers couldn't wait to report such a find to their boxing instructor, Larry Foley, who duly watched the lithe athlete in action. Foley predicted he would make him champion of Australia in a year. Peter Jackson proved his mentor wrong by making it in six months, but imagine the excitement years later of Sammy Woods, one of the brothers, as he watched Jackson pound fellow Australian Frank Slavin to defeat for the World Heavyweight Championship in London, in 1892.

Born at Glenfield, near Sydney in 1867, Samuel Moses James Woods had attended Sydney Grammar School before progressing to the Royston College. In more senior circles he soon excelled at cricket with 1883 as a special year, when capturing 70 victims at an average of five runs each: he took seven in seven balls once. The same year he was brought to England where he was enrolled at Brighton College in 1885 with his younger brother, H. D. L.—Sammy thought he was one of a family of 13 or 14! He is still recognised as one of the fastest school-boy bowlers ever, and with G. L. Wilson was one of the outstanding two Public School cricketers of his time. In his first year he claimed 78 victims, while the next season 14 Lancing College batsmen were all bowled by Sammy in one match.

The natural progression, surely, was for Sammy Woods to go straight to university, but this was momentarily delayed while he tried, unsuccessfully to make 'head or tails' of banking. His failure to achieve a footing in this sphere was probably due to his constant

S. M. J. Woods

absence through playing cricket. Natural progression to university for someone following such a redoubtable early education seems obvious, but in Sammy's case perhaps there were grounds for reconsideration. Going up to Jesus College, Cambridge, in 1888 he had, within a few weeks, made certain of his Blue. A hat-trick in the game against C. I. Thornton's XI helped. It was to be a busy season with a call to play his first Gents versus Players game at Lords, where he captured 10 players' wickets for 76 runs. Although Oxford University were saved by rain, it was not before Sammy had dismissed six of them for 48 runs in their only innings; they were not to be so fortunate in the next three encounters. The Australians were touring here that year, and called on Sammy's services in the three Tests, but he achieved little of note. Perhaps we can return now to the academic requirements expected of under graduates that, in Sammy's case, were conspicious by their absence. Whilst at Cambridge, no one ever read less for, or wrote less in examinations that Sammy. Often he just stayed the mandatory thirty minutes in the examination room, before leaving. He used part of that time to write his name and college at the top of the paper—there was a mistake in that once! For the rest he simply frowned and chewed his pencil. His simple signature shows a distinct labouring to complete.

Although Sammy didn't perform well with the bat in the remaining three Varsity games, he did take his bowling tally to 36 wickets at just under nine runs each. He headed the University bowling averages for all four years, and G. L. Wilson's 53 in 1891 was the only half century registered against Cambridge during that period. Such was the scourge of S. M. J. Woods on the dark blues that they themselves voiced doubts of success if he played. No Oxford innings reached 200 when Sammy played. Probably his most memorable match was the Varsity game of 1890 when he was made captain of the light blues prior to their seven wicket victory. Sammy awarded F. S. Jackson his Blue in the Yorkshire game shortly before that match, because he couldn't bear to see such a talented player worry so over such a certainty.

With Sammy's vibrant spirit and love of the game no match ever went to sleep, when he participated. Bowling at a furious pace and with his Cantab friend Gregor MacGregor standing over the stumps to effortlessly take them was, Sir Pelman Warner recalled, one of the outstanding sights of the game. MacGregor seemed to place his gloves quietly by the off stump and Sammy's deliveries pounded into them as if drawn by some magnetic force. Even after MacGregor was miraculously unhurt following a nudge through a plate glass window from Sammy during a boisterous rag, they always remained firm friends. In the future cricket was to gain tremendously from Sammy's wonderfully happy outlook. He would sometimes revert to bowling lobs, mischeviously quipping how he preferred that style anyway!

Of his 190 wickets while at Cambridge University, perhaps his annihilation of C. I. Thornton's XI at Fenners, in 1890, was the highlight. After taking 5–19 in their first knock, Sammy claimed all 10 in the second for 69 runs—plus a fingernail from the opposing skipper's left hand, because of the latter's refusal to wear a glove! Not a bad effort really when considering Sammy and MacGregor had tried to lure their opponents to a breakfast that morning of strong ale and hot lobsters, so typical of such riotously high living of the times. The two light blues, following a polite refusal by their guests, finished off the lot, only to top it all with a cigar each! Surely the sight all Cambridge followers will remember with relish was when Sammy, with this team needing one run off the last ball to win the 1891 encounter, ran from the Lords pavilion with no pads, no gloves and a hurriedly borrowed bat, smashed the ball to the boundary, and ran back!

As early as 1887, Sammy Woods played regularly for Somerset. This master of practical jokes and story teller of humorous tales fitted into county life immediately, and was the predecessor of several other Aussies to play for that county later. He stood 6′1″ and weighed 13½ stones, a physique of rippling muscle that C. B. Fry enthused about after sharing a cricket ground dressing room with Sammy. For such a giant, Sammy's soft hearted nature made him a favourite with the most down to earth of Taunton's fans. He thought nothing of walking from his Bridgwater home to the Taunton ground on match days. These journeys would entail calling at various farms of friends, and chatting to may passers by. Cricket author, R. C. Robertson Glasgow tells how he went on walks around Taunton with Sammy when the former was a budding Somerset cricketer, and the latter his formidable skipper. The author was intrigued by Sammy's knowledge of local streets and alleys, where he always popped into shops and cottages to enquire of the childrens' health or, possibly, the parents' job prospects.

Sammy Woods loved this Somerset life, and soon settled into the pleasant country ambience of the Taunton county ground. Many was the time he must have played to the accompanying cattle choruses from the nearby market, while at the opposite end of the ground from the pavilion the River Tone beckoned temptingly to his adventurous spirit for a gambled big hit. He was to become a firm favourite, even to his voice acquiring a pleasant rustic lilt to almost replace his more naturally rolling Australian one. He was accepted as one of their own.

He took a wicket with his first county cricket delivery in 1886. The unfortunate victim was Warwickshire's C. W. Rock, who was brilliantly stumped by A. E. Newton from a yorker outside the off stump. Sammy was lucky to have such outstanding wicket keepers for Somerset as Newton and 'Bishop' Wickham, who believed in standing up to everything in the style of MacGregor. Rock was the first of Sammy's 554 wickets for Somerset. Using a high action and strong follow through. Sammy mixed his pace with devastating 'yorkers', and a deceptive change of pace. He learnt the latter art by watching George Lohmann of Surrey and Australia's own 'Demon' Spofforth, whereupon Sir Pelman Warner described him as "the most artistic and subtle fast bowler there has been." Perhaps 'Plum' was remembering the occasion when, as a cringing schoolboy, he hit Sammy's first delivery for four, through the covers. "Well hit, little fellow." Sammy called out before shattering the stumps with the next ball. Overall, Sammy Woods took well over 1,000 wickets, including 100 wickets in a season, twice. During one Somerset game, skipper H. T. Hewett, 'The General', admonished Sammy for straying down the leg side and refused to place a fielder there. When the bowler erred again, four years later, the same captain ranted, "didn't I tell you to keep off that side!" Sammy Woods said he learned a lot about the art of fast bowling from that experience. During one county match Gilbert Jessop tells how Sammy was asked to bowl at a particularly obdurate rustic, who seemed set on survival by blocking every ball. Slowly measuring his run, Sammy turned and enquired of the timorous receiver, "Will you have it over the heart, or over the head!" The striker was run out the same over after taking a suicidal single. Sammy recalls how his elder brother, nicknamed 'Stringy Bark' and left in Australia, was even faster than himself, but less accurate. The M.C.C. touring party, led by Archie MacLaren, vouched for these facts when facing 'Stringy Bark' in the Sydney nets, as he broke or cracked supporting posts of adjoining nets.

Sammy Woods could account for himself well in any fielding position but he specialised as a fearless silly point, while at cover and extra cover he thought nothing of stopping drives with his shins if unable to get his hands there in time. He possessed safe hands as his record of 282 catches denotes. Always a useful batsman, Sammy really came into his own later in life when his bowling pace receded, from about 1893. Being noted as a powerful on-driver didn't detract from his prowess to defend stubbornly, when the occasion called for such tactics. Using his great reach, and strength of shoulder and arm, he would punish good length bowling, not to mention dabbling with the challenge of the 'draw' shot between legs and wicket. His 12,600 runs from 299 appearances for the county included 18 centuries (three before lunch), and 1,000 runs in a season four times. With V. T. Hill as his partner in the game with Kent at Taunton in 1898, he helped to set a seventh wicket county record of 240 runs. How he must have enjoyed his highest score of 215 against Sussex in 1895, at Hove. These he made out of 282 put on in 2½ hours. In the match before, he had amassed 109 at Lords, against Middlesex. Three years after his Hove triumph he made the Sussex bowlers suffer again to the tune of 143, scored out of 173, in two and a quarter hours. He put on another hard hitting display in 1901 with his friend Gilbert Jessop at Bristol. They put on 50 in eight minutes, 100 in 16 minutes and, eventually, 142 in only 22 minutes!

It was in 1894 that Sammy started his thirteen year period of the Somerset captaincy. Such a watchful skipper of opposing batsmens' faults coupled with his extraordinarily pleasant nature, made him a popular figure and welcome in cricket circles. His outlook was typified by his remark that "draws were of no use—except for bathing!" If such a result could be avoided by exceptional tactics, he was not averse to using them. His jutting chin would be set to challenge any crucial situation, while his refusal to be beaten never caused him to try underhand dodges in order to reverse an impending defeat. As skipper of the Gents in 1900 his gesture to bowl another over on 6.30 p. m. after the Players were one run short of their 500 plus total to win, upset the M.C.C. Committee because the action openly flouted the rules. Their huffing and puffing had no effect on Sammy as a satisfactory and thoroughly deserved result had been achieved. He proved himself one of the top county skippers of his time, but the light hearted vein never left him. Up until the Second World War Somerset has been noted for its summer vacating schoolmasters, and young public school boys in radiant caps, dominating the Somerset teams. Gilbert Jessop asked him why one such youngster was playing in the current match between Somerset and Gloucestershire. With a sly smile Sammy pointed out that the unfortunate individual couldn't bat or bowl, he was less of a fielder, but he did happen to be one hell of a golfer! Sammy Woods often rued the fact that Lord Hawke could write down the names of twelve Yorkshire players, on the first day of May, and still have them in July. Sammy would have a list of 50!

Sammy Woods' cricketing expertise, together with his kind nature and zest for the game, made him one of the first choices to be pencilled in by most tour organisers. He visited the West Indies, America twice and Canada, but jokingly remembered how he made only .0012 of a run per mile on his second trip to America! His Somerset average that summer of 1899 had been 40. When touring

South Africa with Lord Hawke's side, in 1895–6, he was selected for the three Tests, thus joining Billy Murdock and John Ferris as Australian Test players who also represented England. As this trio only played against South Africa Billy Midwinter still remains the sole player to represent both England and Australia, when in opposition.

No Gents side was complete without Sammy's name high on the list. From 16 games he captured 75 of the Players' wickets at a cost of nearly 20 runs each, and a prodigious number of overs. In 1894 Sammy Woods and F. S. Jackson bowled unchanged through both knocks to claim an innings victory for the Gents, a bowling record never to be equalled. Of his many friends W. G. Grace was a bit special. Sammy loved to play under the leadership of his idol when the amateurs opposed the professionals in their annual battles. To illustrate the high regard Sammy had for W.G. we have to jump ahead to the year 1925 and the August game of Somerset v Surrey at Taunton. Sammy watched excitedly as Jack Hobbs scored a century in the first innings to equal Grace's record number of centuries, only to make another in the second knock to set a new record of 127. In Sammy's view it had been the highlight of his career 30 years before when he bowled W. G. Grace that easy legside delivery at Bristol, to reach his 126th century: for Sammy the 'old man' would always remain his champion.

Somerset gained first class status in 1891, a factor which Sammy Woods had no small hand in. The two top championship teams of this era were Yorkshire and Surrey, and often Somerset proved a stumbling block to both of them. Sammy seemed to save his best efforts for these encounters, never more so than the county's six wicket win over the champions Surrey in the year of acceptance. Surrey's last man Sharpe hung in until the last over, when Wood, the non-receiving batsman, pointed out to Sammy how well his partner was doing, considering he only had one eye. The left was the good one Sammy discovered when enquiring, whereupon he bowled the only round-arm delivery of his whole career, and knocked poor Sharpe's off stump out of the ground! Earlier that year Surrey were fore-warned of future encounters when Sammy, playing for Cambridge University, had match figures of 14–163, here again helping to send the county side to a 19 run defeat. Surrey's attack of Richardson, Lohmann and Lockwood was one of the most difficult to score against, and many was the time that Sammy cheekily used the 'draw' shot against them to break up tight field placings. Sammy enjoyed several long innings, and seemed to favour the Oval to his own Taunton wicket to make them on. Surrey didn't win at Taunton between 1894 and 1898.

In that same inaugural year, Somerset trounced Yorkshire at Bradford, by six wickets, helped by Sammy's responsible innings of 50, and bowling analyses of 5–62 and 6–64. The following season, at Sheffield, it was another win for the underdogs, by 87 runs, and again, mainly due to Sammy Woods hammering a top score of 76. He was heard to iterate on the difficulties entailed to cope with George Hirst's outstanding swerve bowling. "How the devil can you play a ball that comes at you like a throw from cover point?", he enthused with, I would think, tongue in cheek! Somerset's greatest victory over the Tykes came 10 years later, when, after being shot out for 87 in the first and piling up 630 in the second, they prospered by 279 runs. The two centurians, Lionel Palairet and Len Braund, in the huge second innings were admirably supported by skipper Sammy's knock of 66, not forgetting his 46 in the first, and how the Yorkshire followers loved it. They cheered themselves hoarse, and Sammy's cab was trapped in the throng for 10 minutes, but it didn't matter. The winning captain was speechless, until eventually staggering to the bar of the Queen's Hotel and gasping "champ. . . pagne".

Yes, Sammy did like the occasional tipple, preferably Scotch. Perhaps he acquired the taste from the many harvest suppers he attended, not to mention the numerous matches he played for various farmers' elevens. His after dinner singing of songs was always welcome at any function. Although he partook of whisky, he never advocated its good qualities to youngsters; he suggested they would find ale more appropriate! The Somerset committee, and John Daniel who succeeded him as captain, had some reservations upon his example—but they could never question his performance. In his latter playing days, Sammy was a martyr to rheumatism, which caused him much suffering in later life: he often massaged a little Scotch into his painful joints—just a little! Sammy always claimed that the rheumatism settled into the weakness left following a broken leg sustained in a camel fall during his distinguished World War I Dardenelles campaign service with the Devon Regiment and the Somerset Light Infantry—who else!

As a young man he had proved competent at many sports, even to representing Somerset at skittles, hockey, billiards, rugby and bowls. He loved all forms of exercise from playing golf with his many cricketing friends to walking the Quantocks while following the hounds. Many friends—in conversation he always referred to each of them as "m'dear"—were startled to see him dive at a grass tussock under a bank to a hidden cache, containing bottles of beer. He placed these reserves on previous walks, for future reference! In winter's gloomy days of early darkness he concentrated on billiards, often relating to playing friends of his many visits to London halls to watch the top players, while with Somerset in the capital. Many a fairground boxing booth bruiser was surprised by Sammy, because those early tips from Peter Jackson had never been forgotten. Winter daylight hours were spent turning out for the Corinthian soccer team as a full back, for he had gained a soccer Blue at Cambridge, and had represented Sussex, at county level. If cricket was Sammy's first love, rugger had to be a close second. After receiving his rugger Blue in 1888 there followed 13 caps for England as wing forward, and what an awsome figure he presented in the 'loose' with his strength and speed—he could run 100 yards in 11 seconds.

Sammy Woods continued to be a good servant to Somerset cricket, following his final top class game in 1910. He took on the Secretary's task until 1923, and such was his popularity that any letter with just 'Mr. Sam' for an address never failed to reach him! For 37 years his efforts for the county were a labour of love. How he enjoyed sitting among the popular seats at Taunton when his playing days were finished, still with no head-wear—something he always shunned—and still mingling with his favourite people. That deep voice could be heard to call "Well hit, Sir", or "sit down, there" to an unfortunate non thinker as he crossed the sightscreen, with immediate results! How many of those fellow spectators could remember their poorer upbringings in the village of Burnham, and Sammy's former home? How many could remember jostling their mates to hold Sammy's hand when walking down the street with him? I would bet most could recall being taken to his home for a hot breakfast on Saturday mornings. A certain rather sedate, elderly lady that R. C. Robertson-Glasgow met while travelling in a railway carriage a short way from Taunton, certainly never forgot him. In less than five minutes the subject had reached Sammy Woods, whereupon the lady reminisced on the time she attended a dance as an eighteen year old, and the last order imparted by her parents was not to dance with Sammy Woods. Following a guarded giggle and a faraway look in her eyes, she confided "But I did!"

On April 30th, at the beginning of the 1931 season, Sammy Woods passed away at Taunton. Two ex-Somerset players, Rev. R. E. Spurway and Precundary A. P. 'Bishop' Wickham, conducted his burial service at St. Mary's church, just within bat on ball sound from the Taunton wicket. The church overflowed with many of his playing and non-playing friends, because they were saying a reverend farewell to a fellow lover of country life and sport, and a Somerset institution—they ever after worshipped his memory.

CHAPTER NINETEEN

Robert Abel
(England & Surrey) 1857–1936

JACK Hobbs was an England and Surrey favourite who never hid his light under any bushel. His prowess and masterful batting followed him everywhere he travelled, and such talents he shared and displayed to cricket followers the world over. Bobby Abel, on the other hand, seemed to save the best knocks for the Oval faithfuls, who habitually responded with calls of "Bob, Bob, Bob", at the pavilion rails at the close of play. They sustained the chanting until their diminutive idol shyly came forward on to the balcony to acknowledge their cheers.

They hadn't always been times of happy success for Bobby Abel with Surrey, for after being noticed as a good fielder, and useful bowler, with Southwark Park Cricket Club, Surrey engaged him simply to perform at his best in these two departments. He joined Surrey in 1881, but found the step into top cricket very hard and demanding. It wasn't until three years later that he started to make giant strides towards conquering his inadequacies in coping with the extra pace and accuracy of opposition bowlers.

Abel made his initial breakthrough against the touring Australians in 1886, when compiling an impressive 144 runs. This, perhaps, was the Oval crowd's first opportunity to show their appreciation of the opening batsman's progress, for they made a collection of £68.4.0d. No doubt they also recognised in Bobby Abel a small part of their cockney selves, for he was born at Rotherhithe, on November 30, 1857—a true Londoner. It wasn't long before they nicknamed him "The Guv'nor".

Standing just 5'4", and weighing 10 stones, opening batsmen didn't come much smaller than Abel, (he could have been the original Ovaltiny). When approaching the wickets with his partners he sometimes caused a smile, for the difference in stature was remarkable. For the Players he opened with George Ulyett (nearly six feet tall), William Gunn (6'3"), also John Tunnicliffe and Albert Ward, both

Robert Abel

well over six feet. When walking out with the bulky W. G. Grace for England, the pair looked like father and son. Bobby Abel's regular Surrey partner was Tom Hayward, another giant at six feet plus. Such unusual instances of height differential were not helped by Abel's pronounced waddling gait.

The popularity of this little man among his fellow players was boundless, although he seldom smiled when at the wicket, and his face often carried a serious expression, Abel's modestly, unassuming nature, and ever-pleasing personality, made him one of the most popular professionals of his time. Another aspect was his kindness in never refusing his autographs to any diffident youngsters.

It took hours of dedicated hard graft to make himself into a proficient close-to-the-wicket fielder, especially at slip. He once took six catches in a match against Derbyshire at Derby, 1884. Playing at Portsmouth, against Hampshire, in 1898, he 'pouched' five in an innings. His useful round-arm off-breaks were seldom needed with Surrey's splendid all round attack of Lohmann, Lockwood and Richardson, but he was known to break up many a stubborn partnership. In Surrey's championship year of 1887, Abel dismissed six Derbyshire batsmen for 15 runs. To complete his allround usefulness to Surrey he often took over the gloves when 'keeper Harry Wood was injured.

Of course, it was as an opening batsman that Bobby Abel will be remembered. Using endless patience and thoughtful defence, he could defend stubbornly when the occasion called for such measures, but using his large hands and supple wrists, he could cut and drive furiously. Seldom lifting the ball off the ground, his on-side play was unique. With deft footwork and judgement of length and pace honed to perfection, he amassed runs at the rate they were required, as his record shows. He raced to a century before lunch one day at the Oval. Bobby Abel was regularly criticized for playing shots with his bat off perpendicular, especially against the speed of Kortright, Bradley, Sammy Woods, Mold and Ernest Jones, the Australian. Such accusations of retreating to square leg could hardly be justified when comparing the numerous runs he scored off these quickies over the years. Indeed, Kortright considered him one of the most difficult batsmen to bowl against. Lord Hawke and Gilbert Jessop both absolutely refuted the allegations of "walking" levelled at Abel. Harry Altham, writing in reflective mood, remembered seeing Bobby Abel face Kortright, wearing a bow tie! Another story condusive to Abel's apprehension of fast bowling came after the ageing Surrey star chided a youngster who retreated and lost his wicket. Dejectedly, the lad couldn't contain his emotion. "Of course, you din't back away,

Mr. Abel." "Yes, I did," said Abel good naturedly, and observing the distress his remark had caused continued, "the only difference was the fact that I left my bat there!" In the hands of an artist the bat doesn't always have to be straight, as was the case with Patsy Hendren.

For someone supposedly timid of quick bowling, let us look at his Surrey record. After making his maiden century (110) against Gloucester at the Oval, in 1886, a match incidentally, played at Easter as an experiment, he went on to make 63 others, and eight times he passed the 200 mark. These included massive knocks of 250 v Warwickshire in 1897, 231 against Essex in 1896 and 221 against Worcestershire in 1900—all these innings' were made at the Oval. His highest knock was one of 357 not out against Somerset, on a May day, in 1899, again, needless to say, at the Oval. This was to remain a record until Archie MacLaren surpassed it in 1895 with a prodigious innings of 424, and the luckless sufferers were again Somerset. At the time of Abel's record-breaking effort Surrey rewarded him with £5 because no-one had carried his bat in such a large total (811), but when the Committee decided that £1 per 50 runs, with £5 the limit, was sufficient from then on, Bobby Abel said he would never go beyond 250 again—and he never did!

Bobby Abel's lengthy partnerships for his county are legendary, but here are just a few instances which reveal a consistently high-scoring technique, and again all secured on his home wickets:

379 for 1st wicket with Brockwell v Hampshire, 1897
364 for 1st wicket with D. L. A. Jephson v Derbyshire, 1900
306 for 3rd wicket with F. C. Holland v Cambridge United, 1895
448 for 4th wicket with T. W. Hayward v Yorkshire, 1899
334 for 4th wicket with T. W. Hayward v Somerset, 1899
287 for 5th wicket with W. H. Lockwood v Lancashire, 1899

The memorable stand of 1899 against Yorkshire was in a Surrey total of 551–7 after their opponents had amassed 704. This was a world record for 50 years, and still remains a 4th wicket record in English Cricket. Bobby Abel and Tom Hayward finished with scores of 193 and 273 respectively. There were other opening stands of over 200 runs through the years, and how the Oval crowds bayed when Abel called for his sun-hat, for they knew that he felt like making runs when discarding his faded, but favourite Surrey cap for the wider brimmed one. His partner, Tom Hayward, usually moved his chocolate coloured county cap more to the back of his head, the hotter he became.

In appearance, Bobby Abel could best be described as a sandy haired Dr. Crippen! When 'Shrimp' Leveson Gower jokingly remarked that he should be kept out of sight while the doctor's murder trial ran its course at the Old Bailey, the Surrey star became so worried that he complied with the suggestion. Abel's slightly bulbous eyes and bushy moustache enhanced the likeness. Bobby Abel's fitness was never questioned, but Herbert Strudwick, Surrey's eminent 'keeper, recalled the puzzling fact that even after a mammoth score, the opening batsman showed no sign of perspiring. Another observation the old wicket-keeper mentioned concerned Abel's appetite for run-making, and a dislike of losing his wicket. He had seen Bobby Abel return to the pavilion and practice in front of a mirror the shot he was dismissed by, even after scoring over 200! Once when Strudwick had made a gift of his wicket in a vast Surrey score, Abel pointed out the possibility of making a high score on such a track, if he had stayed. This outlook is not surprising when looking at Abel's achievements for his county. From his 514 games he reached over 1,000 runs in a season eight times, and over 2,000 on four occasions, giving a total of well over 27,000 runs. Only Jack Hobbs, Tom Hayward, Herbert Strudwick and Andy Sandham played more games for Surrey, and Bobby Abel ranks as one of Surrey's greatest, along with Hobbs, Hayward, Walter Read and Jupp up to the 1930's.

Of Abel's 34 games for the Players, his preference for the Oval fixture is quite noticeable. He did play in some of the Lords games, but it was a well known fact that he disliked playing at Headquarters. Incidentally, Canterbury was another ground he never relished, but this, apparently, was for superstitious reasons—he was certainly an enigma. To illustrate further Abel's prodigious run-making capacity at the Oval, a glance at his scores there for the Player's will suffice. In 1894 he made 168 followed by 195 in 1899. This last game will be remembered for the Gentlemen scoring over 300 in each innings, but still losing by an innings. In 1900 he narrowly missed a century at Lords, but was probably still tired from scoring 153 not out in the fixture on his home pitch, the week before. The following year he set a record for the Gents v Players when making 257, and this was to last until Jack Hobbs surpassed it at Scarborough, in 1925, with 266. Bobby Abel must have gained much pleasure when captaining the Players on a few occasions.

Bobby Abel made his home Test debut at Lords in 1888, this being the first of a three match series. He top scored in England's innings victory with 70 in the Second Test at the Oval. His next home Tests were another triple game series in 1896 where at Lords, he again made the most runs in England's first innings, with a solid 94. The 'Might Atom' of Surrey was not averse to sticking out for the pro's rights when it came down to monetary awards. The year 1896 will be remembered for five professionals, namely Abel, Hayward, Lohmann, Richardonn and Gunn, deciding to 'strike' before the Oval Test on the grounds that the Test Match fee should be raised from £10 to £20. When the Surrey Committee agreed to consider their claim Abel, Hayward and Lohmann relented and played. The result was a massive fillip for pro' cricket when the demand for an in increase in Test fees was accepted, and duly paid.

Abel's first Australian visit was with G. F. Vernon's team in 1887-8 where he totalled 320 runs from eight matches. In the winter if 1888-9 Major R. Gardner Wharton took a side to South Africa, which Sir Aubrey C. Smith skippered, and the first two Test matches were played between the countries. In the second at Cape Town Bobby Abel scored 120 in England's win by an innings, and so became the first century-maker in Tests between South Africa and England. After other outstanding knocks, Abel brought home many gifts and various sums of prize money. He scored over 1,000 runs and averaged 48, more than double the aggregate and average of any other tourist. Bobby Abel made his third and final tour with Lord Sheffield's side to Australia in 1891-2. On this trip he finished second to skipper W. G. Grace in the averages with a total of nearly 400 runs at 38 per innings. In the second of the three Tests Abel carried his bat for 132 not out, for which he received a cheque from Lord Sheffield for £50. Bobby Abel could have gone to Australia yet again, with A. E. Stoddard's team in 1894, but would not accept the normal £300 plus expenses—he wanted £500.

In all first class cricket Bobby Abel was always in the top flight. In eight seasons from 1895 to 1902 he topped the 2,000 run mark, while his averages ranged from 41 to 56. His highest aggregate came in 1901 with well over 3,000 runs, and included 12 centuries, made at the age of 42. The year 1888 boasted one of the wettest summers ever, but that didn't stop Abel from making over 1,300 runs, and proving himself the best pro' bat of the year. He made over 1,000 runs in a season 14 times. Bobby Abel's 32,600 runs in a first-class cricket included 74 centuries, and he carried his bat on nine occasions. His 263 wickets may be surprising, because we see so little evidence, but his 492 catches do not come as a shock when remembering his large hands.

When Joe Darling's Australians played Surrey at the Oval, in 1909, they scored 296 for five wickets, but the home side were then caught on a 'sticky' after heavy rain. Surrey were skittled for 96 and 122, but

Bobby Abel used uncanny judgement in selecting which balls to play from those to leave alone. His scores of 34 and 36 were worth many more considering the conditions. In the return match he made an impressive 104 against the might of Howell and Saunders. These performances are more remarkable when considering the batsman's handicap of impaired vision.

After a serious eye infection in 1893 Bobby Abel had to battle with failing eyesight for the rest of his life. Even during his last Surrey match against Somerset at Taunton, in 1904, Bobby Abel looked positively all at sea. His was a sad farewell, and it was distressing for his fellow players and supporters to see him resort to spectacles on this unhappy occasion. They must have recalled those halcyon years from 1895 to 1902 with great affection and admiration, and how gratified they were to remember their idol's benefit match against Yorkshire at his beloved Oval in 1895. Although rain caused the middle day to be abandoned, they turned up in great numbers to contribute donations amounting to £730. Bobby Abel had asked for the 'Stand' takings to be included in his final sum, but the Committee would not comply with his wishes.

During his final days in the Surrey team, Bobby Abel enjoyed cricketing moments to savour in later life. He had the pleasure of putting on over 100 for the first wicket with the young Jack Jobbs, in a Club and Ground game. He experienced happy times coaching the young Surrey players, the senior pro's of Essex, and the pupils of Dulwich College, but, sadly, his disability enforced him to give up these friendly engagements. Perhaps his proudest days as a spectator were when his sons William John, and Thomas Ernest, both played their first games for Surrey. The former was a valued allrounder from 1909 to 1926, and played 170 games, while T.E. moved on to Glamorgan to find his niche.

Bobby Abel died at his home in Stockwell, quite near to the Oval, on 10 December, 1936, but it would be nice to remember him talking to an old adversary about past encounters, now recalled as dear friends. Such a vignette was enacted in a tiny shop close to the main gates of the Oval. Bobby Abel ran a small sports establishment there and an adjoining cricket bat manufacturing premises, where he produced a very successful model that could only be named—'The Guv'nor'. One day Sammy Woods, Somerset's popular fast bowler, visited this shop, and addressed the small shirt-sleeved figure behind the counter who was replacing a box on to a shelf. "Hello, Bobby, how are you?" the kindly giant asked. Turning, and peering more closely through his thick glasses, the old Surrey champion smiled when realising who stood there on the other side of the counter, and moved round to meet him. "Lor' it's Mister Sam, and the times you have nearly knocked my head off is wonderful, isn't it?" Putting a massive arm around the little man's stooped shoulders, Sammy Woods replied in his typically affectionate manner. "Yes, M'dear, and the times you have made my shoulder ache is also wonderful!" Of such stories has the essence of cricket been compounded.

CHAPTER TWENTY

A. J. Webbe
(Middlesex) 1855–1941

THROUGH the ages, the game of cricket has been fortunate in producing retired players who are willing to give their all in administration at the highest level. It never possessed a more dedicated disciple than Alexander Josiah Webbe, whose friendly nature, and jovial approach, continued the good work of I. D. Walker, and his brothers—for Middlesex in particular. Born in London on January 16th, 1855, A. J. Webbe was to make his mark on the cricket pitches at Harrow, as an opening bat of high promise.

Although he and older brother G.A. played in representative games for Harrow, the latter, due to ill-health, was unable to make the full school eleven. This honour fell to A.J. in 1872, and Haygarth's M.C.C. Cricket Scores and Biographies describes how the Lords gates were opened at 5 a.m. to admit arriving carriages, but the horses were not allowed inside the ground. Around this period, and even much later, the Eton v Harrow fixture was one of splendidly dressed couples promenading on the outfields during the intervals. On this particular Friday over 16,000 spectators passed through the turnstiles, but members were not included in this total as they didn't pay for entrance on the day. It is recorded that princes and princesses were seen among the crowd, while on Saturday another 11,000 watched the second day's play.

A. J. Webbe was again to enjoy such pomp the following year, and in 1874 he was made captain. The disappointment of being the losing skipper was made more bearable by his two magnificent knocks of 77 and 80 from the respective low totals of 155 and 145. During these encounters, a friendly rivalry blossomed between the celebrated Lyttleton brothers and Webbe, and continued, indeed, through their varsity days, but A.J. played as a colleague with the Hon. Edward and the Hon. Alfred for Middlesex. It is doubtful if Harrow produced a better bat than A. J. Webbe before the advent of F. S. Jackson and Archie Maclaren.

A. J. Webbe

Going up to Trinity College, Oxford, in 1875, it wasn't long before his prowess and fitness was demonstrated in an innings of 299 not out against Exeter College. This was followed by 120 for Oxford University v Gentlemen of England, surely a performance that helped to bring him his Blue as a Freshman that same season. In the Varsity game Webbe put on 86 with T. W. Lang, which proved most valuable when Oxford gained a narrow six run victory. Another winning factor was a superbly judged boundary catch by A. J. Webbe when he dismissed the dangerous looking Hon. A. Lyttleton towards the end of Cambridge's second innings. Although being elected as treasurer of Oxford University cricket Club in 1876, Webbe had to endure a nine wicket defeat when the two sides met. This setback was amended the next year when Oxford gained revenge with a ten wicket win, especially when A. J. Webbe and brother H.R. knocked off the 47 runs needed for victory. Webbe was also the racquets champion that year, and the next, beating Hon. Alfred Lyttleton both times. The roles were reversed later, however, when Alfred took the gold tennis racquet at Lords in 1888, with A.J. the silver. Both varsity captains, W. S. Patterson and A. J. Webbe were invited to represent the Gentlemen, at the Oval in 1877, but the latter made his debut in 1875, and was to play in many of the games against the Players. Cambridge University's huge win in 1878, by 238 runs, was set up with knocks of 53 and 64 by Edward and Alfred Lyttleton respectively, while Edward had the final say by brilliantly catching Webbe when moving from slip to the leg side, and scooping the ball up left handed. It must have been a poignant occasion for A. J. Webbe for he opened the Oxford Innings with his brother H.R., and was to hand over the captaincy to him for the following year.

With reference to A. J. Webbe's inauspicious first appearance for the Gents in 1875 at the Oval, failure was, perhaps, tempered by the fruitition of a secret ambition to open the innings with W. G. Grace. The Lords game followed immediately and was highlighted by a record opening stand for the fixture of 203 in the second innings, after A.J. had collected a duck in the first. This highly acclaimed partnership was achieved on a damp, responsive wicket for the bowlers, with W. G. Grace finishing with 152, and Webbe 65.

A. J. Webbe's stance at the wicket could be described as typically Harrovian, because he adopted the straddled position, similar to that of Gilbert Jessop, and quite crouched. As an opening bat he showed endless patience on bad wickets, using thoughtful defence, and ruthless attack when required. By late wrist movements his placing and timing were magical when forcing the short ball off his body, or when cutting late and square. Like I. D. Walker before him, A. J. loved to use the 'Harrow Drive', a shot described then as one through the covers, while now it is more commonly described as a slash over cover's head! His fielding was exemplary with numerous splendid catches in any fielding position. Perhaps his bowling would best be described as 'a useful change'. Even though his average height and weight carried no physical ascendancy over fellow players, it is obvious from many of their recollections of A. J. Webbe's generous disposition and tactfully proffered advice that he was a giant personality. On odd occasions his comments on the field of play would appear impetuous, but an immediate apology followed if he thought his actions or words had upset someone. These spasmodic outbursts were treated light-heartedly by most recipients.

The name A. J. Webbe has been synonymous with both Lords and Middlesex cricket for many decades, and he was a great power in the county's early years. His first game was in the year he gained his Blue, 1875. This more than promising 20 year old displayed his potential in the second game, when he carried his bat against the might of Nottinghamshire's bowlers to the tune of 97 not out. Such tactics included a mixture of hitting and defence, a style which saw him second in Middlesex's averages at the end of the season. His first opening partner was I. D. Walker, and what a formidable pair they proved, right up to the retirement of the latter. Webbe's next partner was A. E. Stoddart, who remembered his more experienced colleague's encouragement when arriving at Lords as a confused and lonely youngster from Durham. Webbe's shortened christian name of Alec was widely used, but his initiation into the Middlesex team brought with it the nickname of 'Webbie', although this was only used by closed friends. (I know the feeling as myself and members of my family have often been referred to by the same name, in our hertfordshire village of Redbourn).

On a rain-affected wicket at Sheffield, in 1882, Ted Peate, the season's leading bowler, and Bates, shot out Middlesex for 135, even after the openers Walker and Webbe had scored 95 between them. The Londoners were set just 140 to get to win in this low scoring game, but Peate was supreme with second innings figures of 8–32, thus setting up a Yorkshire victory by 20 runs. The only batsman to shine in the game was Webbe, who batted right through Middlesex's second innings for 62 not out, and never looked like getting out. The county were very fortunate to have A.J. to step into the skipper's shoes after I. D. Walker in 1885, for there was never a more natural replacement. He held the post until Gregor Macgregor took over in 1899. The Metropolitan county was served by such batting stars as Stoddart, O'Brien, Ford and Alfred Lyttleton during A. J. Webbe' s playing career at headquarters, but although the latter was probably more restricted in his stroke play than the other great players, he was certainly more consistent. Webbe was always at the centre of the game, whether on the field or off, for his enthusiasm and charming manner made him a favourite with everyone.

Most outstanding cricketers have years when little goes wrong, and can look back to a certain season when everything clicked. A. J. Webbe's was 1887. Scoring over 700 runs for Middlesex, he had two remarkable innings that illustrated well his form and love of batting. The first was against Kent, at Canterbury, when he again carried his bat for 192 not out, but just a week later, against Yorkshire at Huddersfield, he again batted through, on a fiery wicket for his highest ever total of 243 not out. Yorkshire's 'keeper, David Hunter, stood back to take those balls roaring over Webbe's head. Rain caused the third day's play to be abandoned, so the players entertained the crowd with a football match! A. J. Webbe's innings remained a Middlesex record until 1899 when C. M. Wells made 244 versus Notts, at Trent Bridge. That season of 1887, Webbe made over 1200 runs, with an average of 47. Incidentally, those two centuries were the only ones scored by a Middlesex batsman that year.

As well as the more pleasant memories, batsmen recall their disappointing lows, and perhaps A. J. Webbe tried hard to forget his 'king-pair' v Surrey at Lords, in 1892, when George Lohman claimed his wicket with the first ball of each innings. Another haunting occasion was the season before, when Notts visited Lords and the match was dying, with 30 minutes to play and five wickets to fall. Webbe and Stoddart had put on 95 with A.J. looking well set, but Robinson, the Notts skipper, called on Mordecai Sherwin, the 17 stone wicket keeper and Notts County goalkeeper, to bowl a few innocuous overs, in light relief. He proceeded to bowl A.J. immediately, with the others departing four minutes short of the close. This Notts win was greeted with stony silence from the onlookers. The season of 1881 proved another trough as A.J. received a nasty facial injury on a rough wicket at Oxford University, on the Christchurch ground when playing for the Gentlemen of England. It was decided to restart the game on a pitch at the New Ground.

A. J. Webbe's illustrious playing days ended with his appearance against Worcestershire, at Worcester, in 1900. This was to prove his only game that season, but how he performed. He saved Middlesex from defeat when carrying his bat for a chanceless 59 not out in the last innings, on a difficult wicket. A. E. Stoddart also played his last county game that year. Webbe had carried his bat through an innings eight times, seven for Middlesex, and, in a total of over 14,000 first class runs, he made 14 centuries. 'Plum' Warner found him a constant adviser, who he turned to at worrying times. When captain of Middlesex 'Plum' recalled his memorable welcome from A. J. Webbe, when he first played for the county—very much like A. E. Stoddart. The grateful Warner remembered how Webbe talked him out of retiring at the end of the 1919 season, only for both friends to see Middlesex win the title the following year.

Webbe toured only once, and that was when I. D. Walker was asked by the Melbourne Cricket Club to bring a team of 12 amateurs, but the bowling had to be bolstered with the inclusion of the two Yorkshire pro's, George Ulyett and Tom Emmett. The tour didn't prove successful for A. J. Webbe, but he did play in the Melbourne Test, under the leadership of Lord Harris.

Harrow Wanderers were fortunate indeed to have I. D. Walker and A. J. Webbe to arrange tours, and the latter's own eleven had regular fixtures with the Universities. These games proved invaluable to the furtherance, and increasing standards, of their cricket. Although a sufferer of arthritis, and quite crippled by it in later life, A. J. Webbe lived for cricket. His work in administration at Lords proved boundless, for the list of offices he held reflect many hours given up to his beloved cricket. He held the post of Honorary Secretary of Middlesex, and was made President in 1922, following another great friend, R. D. Walker. This position he filled until 'Plum' succeeded him in 1937. Various Middlesex captains, such as F. T. Mann, Haig, Robins, Enthoven and Peebles were all recipients of constructive advice, when it was sought. Many amateur and professional cricketers benefitted from his prodigious knowledge and know-how. He became a member of the M.C.C. Committee as early as 1886, and was a trustee at the time of his death, but, surely, his greatest moment was the Presidency, in 1925. Again he succeeded R. D. Walker.

No man ever devoted more time to the game, but even A. J. Webbe found a few hours to help relieve the sufferings of others, when serving on various hospital committees. His death, on February 19, 1941 occurred at his home, Fulvers Farm, Abinger Hammer, Surrey at the age of 86, and at that time he was the oldest Varsity skipper. A. J. Webbe's services to cricket were marked with his portrait, by Francis Dodd, R. A., gracing the wall of the Long Room at Lords. It was presented by members of the Middlesex County Cricket Club. Webbe had an uncanny knack of remembering faces, even when not seen for long periods, but now all cricket lovers can see his likeness at the centre of world cricket.

CHAPTER TWENTY ONE

Sir C. Aubrey Smith
(England & Sussex) 1863–1948

In the halcyon days of cricket's Golden Age the game's chronicles are studded with such aristocratic names as Lord Hawke, Lord Harris, The Honorable brothers Lyttleton and Sir Stanley Jackson, but no-one played his 'part' better than Charles Aubrey Smith, although he had to wait 'till the second world war to acquire the prefix to his name. To use such a thespian description is not out of place when referring to Aubrey Smith's bearing, for he took his typically English gentleman's demeanour to Hollywood in the early 1930's—together with his love of cricket.

One of the sports' greatest ambassadors was born to a Brighton doctor in the City of London, during July, 1863. As a keen young player he was fortunate to come under the experienced tuition of the ex-Surrey star Julius Caesar. This association was made possible when Aubrey Smith attended Charterhouse, where Caesar was the resident coach. It wasn't long before the eager quick bowler, after sound instruction, was making quite a name for himself in public school games. After these successes it was no surprise when Aubrey Smith went up to St. John's College, Cambridge, and gained his Blue in 1882, as a Freshman.

Following a relatively quiet debut he played three more years in the Varsity game, and apart from taking five second innings Oxford wickets for 57 runs in 1885, his outstanding figures were in 1883 when he and Charles Studd routed the dark blues on a rain-affected wicket. The weather was kind to the Cambridge batsman during their first innings, but kinder still to produce a pitch tailor-made for Studd's medium paced seamers, and Aubrey Smith's quicker off-cutters. With match tallies of 8–99 and 9–106 respectively, these bowlers needed assistance from no-one else. The Varsity match at this time was a popular date in the cricket calendar for not fewer than 21,000 watched on the first day, and the attendance during the match was around 46,000! The brothers Studd dominated the Varsity game in

Sir C. Aubrey Smith

the early '80's with G.B., C.T., and J.E.K. skippering the Cambridge teams during that period. It's a remarkable statistic that all of Aubrey Smith's university matches ended in a seven wickets victory, three for the light blues and one for Oxford. It is also interesting to note that he first became keen on the stage while at Cambridge.

Lord Sheffield proved an influencial benefactor in early Sussex cricket because he employed Nottinghamshire's Alfred Shaw, together with William Mycroft from Derbyshire to coach young aspirants, and to hold trial games around the county. Aubrey Smith was discovered in one of these fixtures. He played the first of his 99 matches for Sussex in the same year as his Cambridge debut. Exciting times, indeed, for a cricket-mad youngster as he rubbed shoulders with batting idols like C.B. Fry, Ranji and Joe Vine. Perhaps Aubrey Smith's hard hitting style as a lower-order batsman could be too easily described as ordinary—even if he wouldn't give up his wicket quietly, but his bowling was certainly more difficult to analyse. To a right handed batsman his run-up commenced from behind mid-off and continued behind the umpire to eventually deliver the ball from round the wicket: thus he was nicknamed 'Round the Corner' Smith!

For fourteen years Sussex followers were entertained by this fair-haired, six feet tall giant. His handsome features with a bushy moustache, and eye-brows to match, provided ideal film star material, while his large eyes, one staring from a firmly fixed monocle, always reflected deep concern and sincerity. Such manly attributes, together with a typically English gentleman's deportment, made him a Sussex favourite, and a slightly type-cast Hollywood certainty. Before embarking on the latter trail he became captain of Sussex in 1887, but it was thought his nature was too amiable to do a proper job. Having seen how low he batted in the order it is probably surprising to see that his highest score was as many as 142, scored against a Hampshire attack at Hove, in 1888. Perhaps the fact that he was one of the fastest runners between the wickets throws some light on the mystery, but sadly, this was to be his only century in first class cricket. Of his 2,300 runs for his country perhaps his eighth wicket partnership with Ranji at Hove, in 1900, stood out as one of his most memorable stays at the wicket. The Indian maestro plundered 202 in three hours from the Middlesex attack on a worn wicket, and of his stand with Aubrey Smith of 88 in 35 minutes, the latter made two!

If Aubrey Smith's batting record and technique was prone to being assessed in a more flippant manner, his bowling certainly was not. Physically very strong he could niggle away using extreme accuracy and unsettling lift, gained from a free, high action. Of his 300 plus wickets in top cricket, his best performance was five wickets for eight runs against his old University at Fenners, in 1885, shortly after going down. How he must have chuckled when playing for the Past and Present of Cambridge University XI as they defeated the 1882 touring Australians, even if George Bonnor did shatter pieces from a wooden sight-screen while hammering 66 runs in 30 minutes! Once, at Eastbourne's Devonshire Park, Aubrey Smith took 17 of the 19 wicket to fall. It could not have been easy for a batsman to fathom his bowling ploys, for having eventually sussed out where the ball would be delivered from, he then had to cope with pacy off-cutters darting in to test his defences. Sir Pelham Warner might have witnessed just such a ball on his first visit to Lords, as an excited thirteen year old. It was the occasion when the M.C.C. met Sussex in 1887, and, before his seat was warm, he remembered vividly Aubrey Smith bowling F. E. Lacey (an eminent M.C.C. Secretary of the future) with a real beauty.

In the Winter of 1887 Aubrey Smith skippered the Lillywhite, Shaw and Shrewsbury side to Australia and New Zealand. This visit was at the kind invitation of the New South Wales Cricket Association, but G. F. Vernon's team was touring there at the same time, and such strange arrangements inevitably proved unlucrative. On arriving home the following spring, Aubrey Smith was selected for the Gentlemen at Lords, and what a game it proved to be. In the Players' first knock Sammy Woods claimed 5–49, while Aubrey Smith took 3–23 off 23 overs. With the Players second innings standing at 71–6, and needing only six runs for victory, 'Nab' Steel, the Gents skipper, threw the ball to Aubrey Smith and aided by Woods, they took the four remaining wickets for just one run! In a low scoring game the Gentlemen snatched an unlikely victory by five runs. Two days later he again represented the Gents at the Oval, where he bowled economically for 3–71 off 41 overs. Three years later he repeated his miserly offerings as the Players amassed 390, but from 38 overs his three victims cost only 78 runs.

It was proving a busy time for Aubrey Smith on the cricket field, for the winter of 1888 saw him as skipper of the first England touring team to South Africa: the team was managed by the Australian born Major R. G. Wharton. This was an experimental tour, to encourage South African cricket, and its success can be measured by the many happy visits that followed. How sad it is that the power of politics seems to undermine so easily the good work of cricket's pioneering ambassadors. Aubrey Smith's side received tremendous hospitality from the South African people, but when it came to travel the players suffered badly from boredom and personal discomfort. Primitive forms of horse drawn carriages and carts were sometimes substituted by waggons drawn by plodding oxen, and of the 146 touring days only 57 were occupied with cricket, while 25 were required purely for travel.

The first Test ever between the two countries was played at Port Elizabeth, and ended in a comfortable eight wicket victory for the tourists. In South Africa's first innings Aubrey Smith claimed 5–19 off 13 overs. Unfortunately he went down with fever shortly after this match, so handed over the leadership to his friend M. P. Bowden, the Surrey 'keeper, who officiated for the second Test and the few remaining fixtures. From a playing point of view Aubrey Smith performed well with 134 victims at a cost of just 7.6 runs each, and this against many teams of odds. But at the end of the tour he and Bowden stayed on to try their luck as a stockbroking partnership in the booming gold and diamond fields around Johannesburg. It wasn't long before Aubrey Smith had spurred cricket enthusiasm around the city, for he became skipper of the famous Wanderers Club, not to mention his captaincy of Transvaal against Kimberley in the first Currie Cup match. He was a tremendous help in initiating this tournament in its early days, also it was obvious how his verve and encouragement had been instrumental in raising the standard of the game in the Union.

Aubrey Smith didn't stay long in South Africa while trying to earn his fortune, for on his return to England he concentrated on his real love–the stage. In his time he had dabbled as a schoolteacher, also as an association football winger for the Old Carthusians and Corinthians, but it was thought his height was a touch too much for the required mobility of that position. He was a keen musician, but in latter life his hearing was impaired, so depriving him of the full pleasure of such a peaceful past-time. Apart from a close friendship with Sir George Bernard Shaw, perhaps his association with Sir George Alexander had more bearing upon his future, as the latter was the impressario of the St. James Theatre. After playing many leading parts at the theatre, Aubrey Smith was soon engaged as Sir George's secretary.

Aubrey Smith's first professional engagement was at Hastings in 1892, thus leading to his debut in London at the Garrick Theatre four years later. He played many roles in silent films, and America soon became his second home. In the 1920's he progressed to the 'talkies', and in 1930 he set up house in Hollywood. Appropriately, it's name was 'Round the Corner', while the smart weather vane was contrived of cricket bats! The list of films he starred in reads like a gazeteer of Hollywood greats, with titles like The Prisoner of Zenda, Clive of India, Trader Horn, Lives of a Bengal Lancer and The Four Feathers. He was now moving in the more sophisticated Hollywood circles and entertaining stars that we could only marvel at on the silver screen, or collect avidly on cigarette cards.

Living at this tempo and in such a racy style didn't curtail Aubrey Smith's love of cricket at all. It wasn't long before he was boosting the flagging Santa Monica Club at Los Angeles with his unquenchable enthusiasm, even to the point where the local Griffith Park pitches were named after him. Very soon, also , he formed a Hollywood XI, and with his strict code of etiquette, and being a stickler for playing to the rules, he provided a perfect example as its captain. Aubrey Smith was the founder of a league in the Hollywood area, and actually talked local authorities into providing the pitches to play on! It was only fitting that he was President of the South California Cricket Association until his death.

Cricket interest blossomed as Aubrey Smith managed to convert such household names as Ronald Colman, Boris Karloff, Clive Brooke, Leslie Howard and Basil Rathbone to the game, while Mary Astor proved a keen supporter and spectator. After touring England, several Australian teams were invited to 'Round the Corner' on their way home, via the United States. Similarly England tourists received the same extravagant hospitality on their return journey from down under. Wally Hammond, Don Bradman and Vic Richardson all recall being taken to the vast Metro-Goldwyn-Mayer studios by their host, and meeting such lovely celebrities as Jean Harlow, Jeanette MacDonald and Myrna Loy. They also told how Aubrey Smith seldom left off his Butterflies C.C. blazer of magenta, mauve and black stripes, when at ease in his Beverley Hills home. As a young man he had been a member of that exclusive club that accepted only boys from Rugby, Charterhouse and Westminster, while ex-Etonians, Harrovians and Wykehamists could also obtain membership. Aubrey Smith would have played for the club with six members of Ivor Bligh's team to Australia in 1883, but he missed the pleasure of the company of B. J. T. Bosanquet, Douglas Jardine, 'Gubby' Allen, Peter May and the young Nawab of Patawdi, later on. His keenness, however, never waned, for he took a touring Hollywood area side to Canada in 1936; not a bad effort when well over 70!

Understandably, Aubrey Smith's eyesight was, by now, not as acute as it used to be, which is probably the reason why he dropped a slip catch in one particular Hollywood game. At Sussex he had, seemingly, telescopic arms to 'pouch' anything within reach, but on this disastrous occasion he summoned his butler, in a loud clear voice, to fetch his spectacles. At the end of the over the said butler marched sedately to his master and delivered the spectacles on a silver salver. Almost immediately the game restarted the bespectacled 'skipper' fumbled another chance. Slowly taking off his glasses, and turning to his neighbour the, by now, uncomfortable wicket-keeper, Aubrey Smith spluttered that the silly ass had brought out his readers!

Aubrey Smith had been made a C.B.E. in 1938, but the final accolade of a knighthood was bestowed upon him in 1944 for his ". . . support of Anglo-American friendship." This great honour was a mark of the energy and effort he exerted while raising funds and materials for the British war effort—he was now in his 82nd year. Due to having a special clause inserted in his film contracts which gave him free time whenever there was a Test Match being played at Lords, Sir Aubrey occasionally returned to his homeland, amid rapturous acclaim. He was never forgotten, as a close friend, Sir Home Gordon, tells of Sir Aubrey's visit here to see Dennis Compton and Bill Edrich slay the South African bowlers during that hot summer of 1947. Sir Home Gordon took his guest back to Sussex to attend Jim Langridge's benefit game at Hove that same year, and such was the reception that police protection was needed for Sir Aubrey from the over affectionate Sussex followers–they hadn't forgotten him!

Sadly this special person passed away at his Beverley Hills home the following year at the great age of 85, and perhaps it is a fitting epitaph when contemplating that cricket has not produced anyone to compare with him since.

CHAPTER TWENTY TWO

Sir Timothy C. O'Brien Third Bart (England & Middlesex) 1861-1948

WITH Middlesex moving into a strong postition, W. G. Grace thought Gloucestershire's cause could be bettered by a spell of negative bowling outside the off stump. Sir Timothy O'Brien, the frustrated receiving batsman and a blue-blooded Irishman used to lording it at Lords, proceeded to reverse-bat the wide deliveries through the slips. When one of these strokes narrowly missed brother E.M.'s head as he took evasive action by lying flat on the turf with the other slips and wicket-keeper, W.G. threatened to take his side from the field if O'Brien did it again. The Bart needed no further encouragement and slammed the next ball likewise, whereupon W. G. Grace carried out his threat and left the bemused batsmen stranded at the wicket to ponder their next move. Thrashing his stumps far and wide Sir Timothy followed the last fielder to the pavilion, and amid the ensuing arguments offered to fight the opposing captain. Eventually peace was restored, but the reverse stroke and the rattling of stumps in frustration is not a modern innovation.

It must be added that such beligerence was not commonplace, but it does illustrate Sir Timothy's forthright thinking, and his capability to carry out his intentions. Apart from his, sometimes, abrasive attitude, Sir Timothy O'Brien was a most popular figure among his fellow players because they recognised his frank vigour and open-mindedness. This extrovert and hard hitting right hand batsman certainly endeared himself to the Lords crowds who revelled in rapid run-getting displays by their Middlesex stars, Stoddart, Webbe and O'Brien in the last decade of the nineteenth century. Even W. G. Grace had a surprisingly high regard for his lordly adversary, for when 'Shrimp' Leveson Gower asked the champion who he regarded as the best batsman after himself, the reply was instantaneous, "Arthur Shrewsbury, that conjuror Ranjitsinhji, then that cricketer of pranks, Timothy O'Brien."

Following his birth in Dublin in the year 1861 there could only

Sir Timothy C. O'Brien Third Bart

have been one possible date for this explosive character to celebrate future birthdays—the fifth of November. Sir Timothy attended Bath's Downside School, a Catholic establishment steeped in Somerset's leisurely ambience, and a spawning ground for good cricketers. Among its most celebrated sons was Maurice Turnbull, an attractive left hand bat for England and Glamorgan, and not forgetting his Welsh international honours at rugger and hockey. Later, Sir Timothy O'Brien moved to the St. Charles College at Notting Hill, thus being qualified to play for Middlesex. It was at this time he had his first game for the county in 1881 as a 19 year old, and as a member of the now defunct Kensington Park Cricket Club. Although his debut was marred when bagging a 'pair' against Gloucestershire, at Lords, he was primarily played as a wicket-keeper, a position he filled on a few occasions until the advent of Gregor MacGregor in 1892.

The year 1884 was perhaps the turning point for Sir Timothy because he went up to Oxford at the age of 23, and it was a well known fact that a cricket Blue was the prime objective. The freshman was not kept waiting long after outstanding knocks in the run up to that year's Varsity game. Oxford University's hopes were given an unexpected fillip when they defeated the touring Australians by seven wickets, a result set up after Sir Timothy had smashed 92 quick runs. A few days later, he made a rapid 72 for the M.C.C. with the tourists again on the receiving end. Having achieved such an overwhelming success against the Aussies' attack it was no surprise when he was asked to play in the Old Trafford Test, and although Spofforth bowled him for a duck in the first innings, his 20 in the second knock helped to stave off defeat. Sir Timothy's selection for this Test was made possible after Lord Harris withdrew from the team because of his differences with the Lancashire committee concerning Crossland's questionable bowling action. At the end of June his Blue duly arrived with Oxford's seven wicket victory over their light blue rivals. Sadly he collected a 'pair', but was more successful with 44 and 28 in the following year's match, even though the result was reversed. A creditable first class aggregate of 1,150 runs at the end of the season signalled the arrival of a new star.

A tall, powerful man, Sir Timothy was to develop into one of England's most attractive batsmen. Anything well up he drove with great strength, but he could square-cut or chop a ball short of a length with consummate ease and timing. He used his height and reach to smother the spinner's skills, while the pull shot brought him many runs on the leg side. Gilbert Jessop noted, and remembered, how Sir Timothy could despatch off the back foot a ball short of driving length, through a packed offside field. One of his greatest strengths was the ability to score quickly on a bad wicket. It was often levelled at him that he was a bad starter, but surely most players were—and are.

His highest score of 202 against Sussex at Hove, in 1895, is still a Middlesex milestone by way of R. Lucas and Sir Timothy putting on 338 runs in 3 hours 20 minutes, for a fifth wicket record. But his finest honour must have been during the annual clash at Lords with Yorkshire, in the year 1889. After being set 280 runs for victory, in a little over three hours, Middlesex still needed 151 with just 90 minutes to go. Imagine the Lords faithfuls excitement as Sir Timothy proceeded to humiliate Peel, Wainwright and Ulyett to the tune of a century in 80 minutes, the last 83 coming in 35 minutes. This four wicket Middlesex victory, with 10 minutes to spare, created a match aggregate record of 1,295 runs, and the crowd called for their idol to appear at the front of the pavilion afterwards.

Such displays of run making and power hitting were not rare at this time. The Tavern at Lords came under fire during the game with Gloucestershire in 1885, when S. W. Scott drove a ball from W. G. Grace through the doorway, from where it rebounded from a wall back on to the grass. It is said how the barmaid was terrified! Shortly after, and not to be outdone, Sir Timothy ondrove a ball from the same bowler through the same entrance, where it smashed some claret glasses. The barmaid's reaction to the second strike is not recorded! When playing for the M.C.C. against Rugby School, Sir Timothy hit a ball over the old grandstand, and out of the ground. This constant battering must have been difficult to bear as often he baited his attackers to break their concentration: a minor example of stately 'sledging'! In most cases the blarney was accepted in the spirit it was intended, and he remained a friend to all. In his autobiography, Sir Pelham Warner describes his Middlesex debut when called to Taunton for the Somerset match of 1894. Arriving in the lounge of the Castle Hotel after travelling from Rugby, the timid youngster was warmly welcomed by his heroes, A. J. Webbe, A. E. R. Stoddart and Sir Timothy—a gesture that remained indelible in 'Plum's' memory. He also remembered how Sir Timothy was 110 not out in the first innings, on a soft wicket, thus aiding Middlesex to a win by 19 runs.

In the field Sir Timothy O'Brien was safe in any position, but he specialised at point, an important post in old field placings. In between wickets falling he loved to practice bowling with both arms, hoping to catch the skipper's eye. He obviously didn't manage it often, because he only took three first class wickets at an average of

103, including that of W. G. Grace once at Cheltenham, much to the old man's chagrin. Another one of his unique habits, this time when arriving at the batting crease, was to stand behind the stumps to check their alignment. This ritual was generally thought to be a habit from his wicket-keeping days.

Captaincy and leadership came to him in various ways. He led Middlesex on several occasions, and Lord Hawke was very impressed with his natural know-how—"if only he wouldn't talk so much!" Sir Timothy captained the Gentlemen of Ireland—he was a leading figure in the Irish game from 1902 to 1907—against his old university, and reminded them of past times with an innings of 167. Following his tour of Australia with G. F. Vernon's team, in 1887–8, he went to South Africa as a member of Lord Hawke's side in 1895. Although Lord Hawke unfortunately had to stand down from the first Test because he hadn't fully recovered from a bout of fever, it proved a proud day indeed for Sir Timothy when given the England captaincy at Port Elizabeth.

Sir Timothy O'Brien was noted for his vitriolic theories of Irish repression by the British Government. Another smouldering discontentment witnessed by fellow players and officials was his seemingly permanent grudge against anything pertaining to Surrey or the Oval. Heaven knows he didn't exactly fail on the relatively small number of occasions he played there. Of his 18 Gents appearances against the Players, his sole Oval game in 1889, produced an innings of 90, with the first 60 coming in even time. For Middlesex, seven years later he hammered Lohmann, Richardson and Lockwood to all parts of the Oval, on a difficult pitch, to the tune of 137. The Surrey committee obviously had reservations about Sir Timothy, especially after their match at Lords, in 1893. Trailing the visitors by 179 runs after the first knock, Stoddart and O'Brien opened with a stand of 228 in 140 minutes for Middlesex. Sir Timothy's 113 again included mischievous reverse batted shots through the slips, off Walter Read's slow lobs. As the dust settled after one such scuffle, a bail was seen to be dislodged, but, with neither umpire having a clear view of how it came to be on the ground, our martinet stated emphatically, "anyway, I'm not going out!" Replacing the offending bail, he prepared to face the next delivery, and so the game proceeded. By the way, Middlesex eventually won by 79 runs! Following another Bank Holiday fracas the Surrey Committee actually barred him from the pavilion precincts, but he outwitted them by gaining entrance with a member—his butler!

Many of the umpiring stories concerning W. G. Grace are compatible with those of Sir Timothy O'Brien. C. I. Thornton tells of a game he played in with the latter at Harston, in Cambridgeshire. Furious at being given out caught behind off his sleeve, Sir Timothy glared at the white coated figure. "That was either a very ignorant decision, or a downright swindle," he snorted. "I guess, Sir," said the smiling official, "it was just a bit of both!" When the M.C.C. met Derbyshire on a July day in 1905, Sir Timothy played a 'walking' shot towards mid-off, who picked up smartly and threw down the wicket. "I'm not running—I'm not running," he squealed, which further flustered the agitated umpire, who gave him not out. The Derbyshire bowlers couldn't have been pleased when Sir Timothy finished with 153!

Sir Timothy O'Brien played his last Middlesex match in 1898, and finished with an aggregate of well over 7,000 runs, including 10 centuries. He topped the county's averages seven times, coming second twice. Up to his retirement from the county game, near the end of the nineteenth century, Sir Timothy was sixth in Middlesex's all time averages with he and Stoddart batting 259 and 293 times respectively. None of the other four had batted on more than 20 occasions. Fittingly, his final first class game was in 1914, in Attleborough, for Lionel Robinson's XI versus his old university. At the age of 53 he treated them to two knocks of 90 and 111, a revelry of stroke play for the young graduates to savour for the rest of their lives.

In latter life he doted on his family of two sons and eight daughters. Such a huge clutch was the result of his marriage in 1885, to Sir Humphrey de Trafford's beautiful daughter Gundrede Annette Teresa. Timothy O'Brien was also made a baronet that year. The eldest son, John Aloysius was killed in action during the First World War, and the baronetcy passed to the youngest, Robert Rollo Gillespie—what lovely family names. Up until his death at Ramsey, on the Isle of Man, in 1948 and aged 87, Sir Timothy O'Brien had been England's senior Test player in matches with Australia. He loved nothing more than to sit in the sun at his beloved Lords to watch Middlesex play, such a simple pleasure for this charitable supporter, and revered personality in his playing days.

CHAPTER TWENTY THREE

Charles Jesse Kortright (Essex) 1871–1952

WINCHESTER will always by synonymous with the name of one of cricket's notable historians and incurable devotees, Harry Altham. For a short while after World War I he played for Hampshire, but for a much longer period he was a well loved classics and housemaster at Winchester College, and Cathedral guide. It was as I gazed at Harry Altham's memorial stone within the hallowed precincts of the cathedral that I was reminded of the occasion when I read his appreciative memories of the game, and their fulfilment. He had fielded to the unique talents of Ranji and Archie MacLaren. He had experienced total joy when being comprehensively bowled by an apologetic Colin Blythe. But, most of all, he had seen W. G. Grace bat . . . and Charles Kortright bowl. In a way such revelations are compatible with the dream of Hugh Cameron, South Africa's gifted wicket keeper in the early 1930's, whose life was cruelly curtailed at an early age by enteric fever. His supreme test of a stumper's ability would have been to keep to the early 'googling' technique of B. J. T. Bosanquet, at one end, while trying to cope with Kortright's blinding pace at the other.

Following such glowing accolades it is difficult to understand why Charles Kortright was never selected for England in a Test match. He almost achieved that recognition in 1899 when England's leading pacemen were injured, but, sadly, he too was incapacitated. At this period the selectors were embarrassed with a battery of top class fast bowlers to pick from. Surrey had Richardson, Lockwood and Knox competing for places against Lancashire's Brearley and Mold, while Warren and Bestwick of Derbyshire kept up the pressure with Fielder of Kent. Even in such exalted company Kortright's extra pace and ferocity was outstanding, which makes his non-selection all the more mystifying.

Charles Jesse Kortright was born at Ingatestone, Essex, in 1871. Growing up in the comfortably affluent surroundings of his land-

155

Charles Jesse Kortright

owning family, the youngster was soon sent to nearby Brentwood School, where he remained until being moved to Tonbridge. As a lad he had aspirations to be a slow right arm bowler, but this unusual obsession for a youngster soon changed as his frame filled out to give extra impetus to his strength and athleticism. He made the Tonbridge elevens in 1887 and 1888, and the following year made his Essex debut. Although the county didn't attain first class status until 1894, Kortright had made a considerable contribution to this end, some years before.

Nothing was wasted in his rhythmic, loose limbed run-up, approaching twenty yards, and standing a generous six feet in height he was able to dig the ball in just short of a length, with unnerving frequency. Kortright claimed that one such delivery, in a club game at Wallingford, disappearred over the keeper's head and boundary for six byes! He presented a ferocious sight as his face twisted in menacing grimaces when releasing the ball, and while playing on rough wickets many of the top batsmen often lost their appetite for runs. Little Bobby Abel, Surrey's star opener, was teased many a time for retreating, but he laughingly explained how he never forgot to leave his bat there. His record against such a battering stood up admirably to all the jibes. On the odd occasions during these biblical encounters when the midget opener was guilty of leaving his post, he explained his actions by having thoughts of his wife and children at home!

When the velocity of bowlers, ancient or modern, is discussed, the comparison is always made with that of Charles Kortright. Such immortals as Sir Stanley Jackson, William Gunn, Gilbert Jessop, Wilfred Rhodes, Sammy Woods, Sir Pelham Warner and C. B. Fry all thought him the quickest of their age, but it is interesting to note that Sir Jack Hobbs considered his Surrey team-mate, Neville Knox, that fraction faster. Neville Cardus once pressed his Lancashire idol, Johnny Tyldesely, to explain what Charles Kortright, or 'Korty' as he was known, actually did with the ball, apart from bowling as fast as he could. Measuring his words carefully, Tyldesely confessed that the Essex quickie did just that, because there wasn't time for anything else! Right from a young man Kortright was blessed with unbounding enthusiasm and stamina. E. H. D. Sewell, a fellow Essex player, tells how when standing at slip to Kortright it was nothing for the bowler to field a ball at point or gully, in his follow-through. His agility for such a big man was quite outstanding.

Whether at Leyton or the Oval, Kortright enjoyed his encounters with Surrey, and seemed to save his best for these games. His duels with Bobby Abel, and the knowledge that Surrey was one of the top counties, all helped to fuel his undying enthusiasm to do well—he would also be playing with, and against, his idol, Tom Richardson. Kortright had match figures of 13–64 in 1893, when he and Walter Mead bowled unchanged through both innings, whilst two years later, and again at Leyton, he took six wickets for four runs, including the scalps of Hayward, Abel and Lohmann. It was during a particularly quick spell one afternoon at the Oval, when Kortright 'yorked' Brockwell with such force that the ball rebounded back past him, almost to the boundary.

It used to be one of the spectacles of cricket when a fast bowler sent a stump cartwheeling through the air, when successful. 'Korty' did it regularly. Essex's 'keeper used to be Tom Russell, father of A. C. 'Jack' Russell, and he never stood nearer than 10 to 15 paces from the batsman's wicket, to take Kortright's deliveries. It was nothing for him to dodge the odd airborne stump, and once at Lords, one flew over his head to stick in the turf behind him! George Giffen, the crack Australian batsman, was once surprised by a short pitched 'flyer' that spun his hat round on his head. He was dismissed next ball, guilty of chatting to the square leg umpire—and he forgot to leave his bat there! Essex was well served by 'Korty' in its initiation into cricket's top flight, and he had considerable influence on the county's worthiness, when being considered. Many leading batsmen were soon to feel the wrath of his endeavours. Being of stern features and rather self centred opinions, his nature tended to inflame certain moments of tension. The mighty Yorkshire side at this period was demolished by him at Leyton, in 1900, to the tune of 8–57, in a demonstration of sheer aggression. This Tykes team only lost two games in three years at this period. Between 1895 and 1898 he took 319 first class wickets, including 226 clean bowled. His best years for the county were in 1895 and 1898 when he claimed 76 and 96 respectively. Against the touring 1893 Australians at Lords he had figures of 8–129, hitting the stumps six times. How he must have wondered what he had to do in order to gain Test selection. Another red-letter day was registered at Southampton, against Hampshire, in 1898, when he finished with six victims at a cost of just ten runs each.

As can be seen, Kortright's value to Essex as its main spearhead of attack was inestimable, but his batting, as menacing in style as his bowling, often rescued the county, or helped put it in a stronger position. This tall right hander strode in around number seven and was capable of despatching any bowler to the boundary, and over it. In fact Essex played him for his batting when his bowling fervour diminished towards the end of his career. Included in a total of well over 4,000 runs in first class cricket were just two centuries, but what beligerent affairs they were. In 1898, at Leicester, the Essex total of 515 (400+ at the end of the first day) contained a century from Bob Carpenter, half centuries from those inseparable 'twins' Perrin and McGahey, followed by 'Korty' chipping in with 112. Two years later Kortright made the Middlesex bowlers suffer at Leyton when compiling a rapid 131 out of 166 put on while at the wicket. In a sixth wicket stand of 117 with E. Russell, the latter contributed a mere 16! Walter Mead must have been pleased with the performances of both men as it was a benefit match. In 1891, before either Essex or Hampshire achieved first class status, 'Korty' entertained the Southampton faithfuls with an innings to remember—158 in one and three quarter hours. When 'resting' in the field he proved more than a useful 'slipper'. For just one season, in 1903, Kortright shouldered the county captaincy.

The last three years of the nineteenth century proved a period of unrest in Kortright's association with Essex. During the early months of 1899 he sustained a mysterious leg injury at home, which caused him to miss all of that season, but to those more closely informed a tiff with the Essex Committee seemed the more likely reason for his absence. The next season was a time of reckoning for those counties possessing bowlers with suspect action, and to Kortright's horror his delivery came under scrutiny. To register his indignation he started to investigate the intrigues of leg-break bowling, only to shock his committee and team-mates by using these tactics in the odd county game when the wicket proved inconducive to fast bowling. It seemed that little niggling things crept into this game. For instance, he thought nothing of rubbing the new ball in the dust to achieve a firmer grip, which dubbed him thoughtless towards his opening partner Walter Mead, who depended more on swing and movement off the wicket. 'Korty's' match figures usually helped to smooth out tense moments in the dressing room after.

With Kortright's temperament dependent on such a short fuse most batsmen tended to placate rather than upset him when facing those lightning deliveries. All it needed to test 'that fuse was for a young aspiring, public school boy batsman to take up his stance with a cocked left toe. Such a preliminary was quite common at this time, but the infuriated Kortright wasted no time in trying to 'york' the offending toe-cap. In 'Korty's' eyes the only batsman to be allowed to get away with this 'offence' to his pride was W. G. Grace himself, whose expertise the bowler was always ready to acclaim as the tops.

Although in Kortright's eyes W. G. Grace's batting expertise was never questioned (Ranji was always his favourite striker), perhaps the 'master's' tactics and code of sportsmanship occasionally left a lot to

be desired. In 1898 Gloucestershire played Essex for the first time
since the latter's initiation into top cricket five seasons before. It
wasn't long before contributory factors to the eventual row started to
show themselves. W.G. had taken a dubious catch in the field, which
Gilbert Jessop, at cover, plainly saw as illegal, but the doctor's
jubilant actions convinced the umpires of its validity. When it came
to the great man's turn to bat, the atmosphere was decidedly icy,
especially when Walter Mead soon caught and bowled him, only for
the batsman to remonstrate with the umpire that it was a bump ball,
and he wasn't going out. It wasn't long before Kortright was beating
the 'unmovable' W. G. Grace with short pitched-deliveries of fright-
ening pace. To the bowler's increasing fury he had a catch behind
and a confident l.b.w. turned down, and when he made contact with
one very fast ball just above the belt buckle of W.G.'s flannels, the
tempers of both men boiled over. The seam was clearly imprinted on
the offended batsman's stomach, and some claimed it was possible to
read the makers name! Shortly after, 'Korty' shattered the doctor's
wicket, and chided the retreating batsman with mock surprise that he
was actually going out when there was one stump still standing! Such
a remark was the last to pass between either of the aggrieved parties
for the rest of the match, and the next few days.

Just nine days later, in fact, the two combatants played on the
same side at Lords when W.G. captained the Gentlemen against the
Players. With the first day being the doctor's fiftieth birthday, well
over 17,000 people attended to register their appreciation (there were
more than 24,000 on the next two days). Such celebrations made it a
poignant occasion, especially as it was Arthur Shrewsbury's last game
for the Players. The animosity between Kortright and his skipper was
still apparent, but the Essex paceman still bowled flat out in a
marathon of 37 overs in the first innings, and another 36 in the
second. This was a tremendous effort considering the match was
played in extreme heat against a Players side that batted all the way
down. In its final innings, the Gentlemen's eleven was faced with a
daunting task on a well-worn wicket, and the achievement of a
respectable draw was going to require a super human effort. On that
final evenings W.G., batting at number nine, due to lameness and a
bruised hand, was joined by last man Kortright with more than 70
minutes left for play, and survival their only target. The pair had put
on 78, but more to the point there was only a minute or two
remaining when 'Korty' succumbed to a Lockwood delivery, and was
caught by Schofield Haig at cover for a top score of 46. It had been
an epic struggle. So much so that W. G. Grace linked arms with his
adversary as they walked off, a gesture widely acclaimed by the

cheering crowd. The heroic pair had to appear on the balcony in answer to their supporters' calls, but more importantly the rift was healed.

Charles Kortright made his debut for the Gents in 1893, at Lords, and it was stylish Archie MacLaren's first game, as well. The Players could only amass 118 in their first innings, and it was Kortright's exceptional pace in taking 7–73 that put them in trouble. Another outstanding feature of the game was the 'keeping of Gregor Mac-Gregor, who was used to standing up to all bowlers, but in the current match was continually forced to stand back because of Korty's aggression. Although not conceding a bye in this innings, MacGregor brought off a stupendous right hand catch, low on the off side while standing up. Probrably the unlucky R. H. Sugg was entitled to feel slightly aggrieved, but not so Johnny Briggs, whose leg stump was sent cartwheeling 17 yards! This display of MacGregor's typified the courageous spirits of wicket keepers of this era. Somerset's Henry Martyn and Bill Storer of Derbyshire were known to stand up to Kortright and other quickies on the rough wickets experienced then.

It was a sad day for charles Kortright and Essex when he played his last game for the county in 1907, but the public were still able to see him perform in top club games with the M.C.C., Stoics, I. Zingari and Free Foresters, the latter club's membership being by invitation only and once referred to as ". . . the most difficult to get into". Even when forced to stop playing his appetite for the game was amply shown in his capacity as a long standing Essex Vice President, and a regular spectator at the county grounds. His summers had always been devoted to cricket, because he was for ever pointing out how little else there was worth doing at that time of the year. At the age of 70 he still retained his slim, angular frame, and was a picture of health. A quiet, Edwardian-type existence with his sister Caroline aided him to retain his fitness throughout.

His love for the countryside was enhanced when walking winter stubble, over which he became a proficient shot. Golf was another out-of-cricket season pastime he participated in, mainly at the Essex club of Thorndon Park, where for years he was a devoted member and, eventually captain. When not actually participating in a sport he loved nothing more than discussing the ethics and laws of his beloved cricket. Following World War I, he held forthright views on many aspects of the game such as condemning the view that those wickets were not conducive to fast bowling; he thought it more a lack of dedication to practice by young fast bowlers. Didn't they now have bigger stumps to bowl at, smaller balls to bowl with, wider creases and umpires empowered to give an l.b.w. to a ball pitching outside the off-stump. It had always been his criterion that a fast bowler's aim was to bowl as fast and as straight as possible, and then strive to bowl even faster. This last target was one he impressed on Ken Farnes, Essex and England's young fast bowling hope who was so tragically killed in the air during the Second World War. He advised the promising youngster to bowl more 'yorkers', and conserve his strength to bowl at great speed directly at the stumps, for longer periods. In the Players first knock at Lords in 1938, Ken Farnes hit the stumps five times in his 8-43, and few of those who faced him had witnessed such pace and aggression before. Old-timers watching were reminded of these halcyon days when his mentor destroyed opponents with the same aptitude. Frank Tyson used the same successful method on the 1955/56 Australian tour when he demoralised the opposition with his direction and velocity.

Charles Kortright died peacefully at South Weald, in Essex, just a week or two short of his eighty-second birthday, and was laid to rest in Fryerning churchyard only a cricket-pitch length from his old Essex playing colleague, A. P. 'Bunny' Lucas. 'Korty' had probably been cricket's speediest bowler, and in his many years of retirement friends would often question those seasons of expounded energy and stress. He dismissed such doubts with a proclamation of their sheer pleasure, and that he had never done a days work in his life!

Selected bibliography

Altham, H. S. & Swanton, E. W. HISTORY OF CRICKET, Geo. Allen & Unwin Ltd., 1926

Ashley-Cooper, F. S., MIDDLESEX COUNTY CRICKET 1900–1920, Wm. Heinemann, 1921

Ashley-Cooper, F. S., NOTTINGHAMSHIRE CRICKET & CRICKETERS, Henry B. Saxton, 1923

Barlow, R. G., FORTY SEASONS OF FIRST CLASS CRICKET, John Heywood Ltd.

Bettesworth, W. A., CHATS ON THE CRICKET FIELD, Merritt & Hatcher, 1910

Box, C., THE ENGLISH GAME OF CRICKET, 'The Field' Office, 1877

Draft, R., KINGS OF CRICKET, J. W. Arrowsmith, 1893

Daft, R., A CRICKETER'S YARNS, Chapman & Hall Ltd., 1926

Ford, W. J., MIDDLESEX COUNTY CRICKET CLUB 1864–1890, Longmans, Green & Co., 1900

French, Lt. Col. The Hon. G., (D.S.O.), THE CORNERSTONE OF ENGLISH CRICKET, Hutchinson & Co.

Fry, C. B., LIFE WORTH LIVING, Eyre & Spottiswoode, 1939

Fry, C. B., (Edited by), THE BOOK OF CRICKET, George Newnes Ltd.

Grace, W. G., CRICKET, J. W. Arrowsmith, 1891

Grace, W. G., W. G.: CRICKET REMINISCENCES & PERSONAL RECOLLECTIONS, James Bowden, 1899

Green, B. (Compiled by), THE WISDEN BOOK OF OBITUARIES 1892–1985, Macdonald Queen Anne Press, 1986

Harris, Hon. G. R. C., THE HISTORY OF KENT COUNTY CRICKET, Eyre & Spottiswoode, 1907

Harris, Hon. G. R. C. & Ashley-Cooper, F. S., LORDS AND THE M.C.C., Herbert Jenkins Ltd., 1920

Harris, Hon. G. R. C., A FEW SHORT RUNS, John Murray, 1921

Hawke, Hon. M. B., RECOLLECTIONS & REMINISCENCES, Williams & Norgate Ltd., 1924

Haygarth, A., M.C.C. CRICKET SCORES & BIOGRAPHIES (VARIOUS VOLS), Longmans & Co., 1876–1879

Hodgson, R. L. ('Country Vicar'), CRICKET MEMORIES, Methuen & Co. Ltd., 1930

Hodgson, R. L. ('Country Vicar'), SECOND INNINGS, Hutchinson & Co. Publishers Ltd., 1933

Hodgson, R. L. ('Country Vicar'), THE HAPPY CRICKETER, Frederick Muller, 1946

Holmes, Rev. R. S., HISTORY OF YORKSHIRE COUNTY CRICKET 1833–1903, Archibald Constable & Co. Ltd., 1904

Kynaston, D., BOBBY ABEL: PROFESSIONAL BATSMAN, Secker & Warburg, 1982

Ledbrooke, A. W., LANCASHIRE COUNTY CRICKET 1864–1953, Phoenix House, 1954

Leverson Gower, Sir H. D. B., OFF AND ON THE FIELD, Stanley Paul, 1953

Lyttelton, Hon. R. H., GIANTS OF THE GAME, Ward, Lock & Co. Ltd.

Martineau, G. D., THEY MADE CRICKET, Museum Press, 1956

Martineau, G. D., THE VALIANT STUMPER, Stanley Paul, 1957

Morrah, P., ALFRED MYNN AND THE CRICKETERS OF HIS TIME, Eyre & Spottiswoode, 1963

Palgrave, L., THE STORY OF THE OVAL, Cornish Brothers Ltd., 1949

Parker, E., THE HISTORY OF CRICKET (The Lonsdale Library), Seeley Service & Co. Ltd.

Pridham, Major C. H. B., THE CHARM OF CRICKET PAST & PRESENT, Herbert Jenkins Ltd., 1949

Pullin, A. W. ('Old Ebor'), OLD ENGLISH CRICKETERS, Blackwood & Sons, 1900

Robertson Glasgow, R. C. 46 NOT OUT, Hollis & Carter, 1948

Ross, G., THE SURREY STORY, Stanley Paul, 1957

Sewell, E. H. D., CRICKET UNDER FIRE, Stanley Paul

Standing, P. C., CRICKET OF TODAY AND YESTERDAY, Two Vols., Blackwood, Lebas & Co., 1902

Thomson, A. A., PAVILIONED IN SPLENDOUR, Museum Press Ltd., 1956

Thomson, A. A., ODD MEN IN, Museum Press Ltd., 1959

Thomson, A. A., CRICKET: THE GOLDEN AGES, Stanley Paul, 1961

Warner, Sir P. F., (Edited by), IMPERIAL CRICKET, The London & Counties Press Assn. Ltd., 1912

Warner, Sir P. F., LORDS, 1787 – 1945, George G. Harrap & Co. Ltd., 1946

Warner, Sir P. F., GENTLEMEN V PLAYERS 1806 – 1949, George G. Harrap & Co. Ltd., 1950

Warner, Sir P. F., LONG INNINGS, George G. Harrap & Co. Ltd., 1951

Woods, S. M. J., MY REMINISCENCES, Chapman & Hall, 1925

'THE CRICKETER' Magazine, Many volumes from volume 1, 1921

ERRATA.

Page	Line	
iii	7	*for* Mynn, *read* Mynn (Kent & England)
vi	7	*for* Criketers, *read* Cricketers
13	38	*for* because, *read* became
44	41	*for* averagesm, *read* averages
46	28	*for* brillian, *read* brilliant
95	42	*for* matter, *read* latter
110	30	*for* member, *read* members
111	9	*for* valuabale, *read* valuable
114	7	*for* old pro and third in line of succession., *read* old pav and second in line of succession.
118	22	*for* pasttime, *read* pastime
118	30	*for* constructive, *read* constructively
139	30	*for* hertfordshire, *read* Hertfordshire
144	34	*for* country, *read* county
159	9	*for* was a benefit match., *read* was his benefit match.